AN INSTANT PLAY‹

THE
THICKNESS
OF
SKIN

CLARE MCINTYRE

**NICK HERN
BOOKS**
London

in association with

**THE ROYAL
COURT THEATRE**
London

The Thickness of Skin was first performed at the Royal Court Theatre Upstairs, London, on 28 March 1996 with the following cast:

LAURA	Amelia Bullmore
MICHAEL	Rupert Frazer
ROANNA	Elizabeth Garvie
IMOGEN/CHRISTINE	Maggie McCarthy
JONATHAN	Toby Ross-Bryant
EDDIE	Mark Strong

Directed by Hettie Macdonald
Designed by Anabel Temple
Lighting designed by Geoff Spain
Sound designed by Paul Arditti

An Instant Playscript

The Thickness of Skin first published in Great Britain in 1996
as a paperback original by Nick Hern Books Ltd,
14 Larden Road, London W3 7ST
in association with the Royal Court Theatre, London.

Reprinted 1999, 2005

Typeset by the author
Re-formatted to publisher's specification by Country Setting, Woodchurch, Kent TN26 3TB
Printed and bound by CLE Print, St Ives, Huntingdon PE27 3LE, Great Britain

ISBN 1 85459 350 1

A CIP catalogue record for this book is available from the British Library

The Cast

MICHAEL   Laura's brother. Roanna's husband.
           Jonathan's father. Mid forties.

ROANNA   Early forties.

JONATHAN.   Seventeen.

LAURA   Early thirties. A secondary school teacher.

EDDIE   An acquaintance of Laura's. Early thirties.

           A Northerner.

IMOGEN   Next door neighbour of Michael and his family.
                    Early forties. A sufferer from schizophrenia.

CHRISTINE   Director of a centre for homeless people.

The play takes place over the winter with Christmas in the middle.

SCENE ONE

Setting: Michael and Roanna's house. What we see of it should suggest a middle-class home belonging to well-heeled people. It is the top floor so there should be the suggestion of a staircase and when people enter and exit they should come up and go down the stairs.

There is a smart ladder going up into the attic. Until indicated in the script there are the sounds of carpentry work emanating from the attic through the open hatch.

Time: A Saturday morning. Beginning of December.

Laura is looking through some things that are sitting on the floor which have just been taken out of the attic.

Roanna enters with some empty black bin liners. She pulls on a pair of rubber gloves. Laura picks up a picture: a framed reproduction.

LAURA. Mum and Dad used to have this at the bottom of the stairs.

Roanna puts some cardboard boxes into a bin liner. These boxes are smallish, shoeboxes and the like and all rather messily tied up with string.

I'm sure that's right. Yes. They did.

PAUSE

Are you sure you don't want it?

ROANNA. (without looking) Absolutely.

LAURA. What about Michael?

ROANNA. Oh take it. Take whatever you want. He'll never know. He hasn't got a clue what's up in the attic.

LAURA. Are you sure?

ROANNA. Yes. I don't know why we've got it all in the first place. They were as much your parents as Michael's. There's no reason why we should have it.

LAURA. I'm not surprised. I bet I turned my nose up at it ten years ago.

ROANNA. Don't take anything if you don't want it. You don't want to get all bunged up with junk like us.

LAURA. Oh I do want it.

ROANNA. Fine.

LAURA. I'll stick it up in the staffroom.

Roanna goes over to the bottom of the ladder and calls up.

5

ROANNA. Jonathan!! (she waits) Where's he gone?

LAURA. I don't know.

ROANNA. God . . . Jonathan!

PAUSE

LAURA. It'll give us something to look at while we stand and drink our coffee: us poor sods that is who've managed to get there too late to get a seat . . . *again.*

ROANNA. I can't *believe* that he's been this stupid.

LAURA. What's the matter?

ROANNA. He's gone and got involved.

LAURA. What do you mean?

ROANNA. All these shoeboxes and business . . . I don't know what: everything in here belongs to this woman Imogen.

LAURA. Who?

ROANNA. The loony lady we've got next door.

LAURA. Oh.

ROANNA. Michael's told you about her hasn't he?

LAURA. Yes he has. I mean, I know about her.

ROANNA. She's got a bedsit or a little flat or something.

LAURA. What does she actually have? I mean . . .

ROANNA. I've no idea. But she's seriously ill. She shouldn't be there at all. And he's gone and put her . . . whatever this load of filthy rubbish is . . . up in our attic. I can't believe it.

She hears someone coming. She calls:

Jonathan.

Michael enters. He is wearing a suit.

MICHAEL. No. Me . . . Laura.

He goes over to Laura. They embrace.

LAURA. Hello.

MICHAEL. How's it all going?

ROANNA. Fine. It's going fine.

MICHAEL. I'm only asking.

LAURA. I'll take these things out to the car. Do you remember this Michael?

She holds up the picture for him to see.

MICHAEL. No.

ROANNA. See? Take it.

Laura exits with a few things.

MICHAEL. What is it?

6

ROANNA. Oh. A picture your parents had.

MICHAEL. No. The mood.

ROANNA. Don't start. It's been a very trying morning.

PAUSE

MICHAEL. What exactly is he doing?

ROANNA. You *know* what he's doing.

MICHAEL. It's a simple question.

ROANNA. He's putting down floorboards where there aren't any. He's putting up some shelves where we haven't got any. He's putting up a work bench // so we can store the bigger . . .

MICHAEL. (interrupts) A work bench! A work bench! Who's going to be doing any work up there? Jonathan? Maybe it's a good idea. Maybe that's what we'll have to do with him to get some results: lock him in the attic tied to the work bench.

ROANNA. It's just a sort of table. A surface.

MICHAEL. What's it for?

ROANNA. We need places to put things, to store things. It's all sitting in a heap up there at the moment.

MICHAEL. So what's this stuff here?

ROANNA. Stuff Laura's having of your parents. And . . . Oh I don't know . . . just the junk you manage to accumulate. But we had to get it out so he had the space to work up there.

MICHAEL. If it's junk why are we paying someone to put up brand spanking new shelves for it all to bloody well sit on?

ROANNA. Just let me get on with it will you? I do know what I'm doing. You don't give the attic a moment's thought from one end of the year to the next. There are things of the girls up there. And Jonathan's. And things I know I don't want to be shot of. And it's high time it was more organised.

PAUSE

MICHAEL. I didn't know until this morning that we were going ahead with this.

ROANNA. Yes you did Michael. You'd forgotten.

MICHAEL. The last time we discussed it it was a 'maybe'.

ROANNA. It wasn't.

MICHAEL. Laura phoned and said there was this chap she knew, some hanger on who's latched onto her no doubt, who was a carpenter and could do everything and did we want him to do anything round the house. And we didn't // make any decision on it.

ROANNA. And *I* said he could do something to sort the loft out a bit.

MICHAEL. Ah. That's when the decision was made.

ROANNA. I wasn't going to let him loose on the house.

7

MICHAEL. Why should we let him do anything? That's what I want to know.

ROANNA. She kept badgering me Michael. You know what your sister's like.

MICHAEL. Inside out.

ROANNA. Well it's done now. There's no harm in it. It really is going to be rather helpful.

MICHAEL. How much am I paying him?

ROANNA. A couple of hundred.

MICHAEL. And have there been any words of thanks?

ROANNA. From Laura?

MICHAEL. Yes.

ROANNA. You're joking.

MICHAEL. She really is very naughty. She'll have a plan for how she's going to help this chap out and nothing's going to stand in her way.

ROANNA. She exploits you.

MICHAEL. Of course she does. But she can't see it. He'll be her latest crusade. And come on: what's two hundred quid?

The carpentry noises stop – unnoticed by them.

Why isn't Jonathan here giving you a hand?

ROANNA. He was here.

MICHAEL. So he's bunked off.

ROANNA. I don't know.

Laura enters.

MICHAEL. So tell us about this carpenter chap.

LAURA. Eddie?

MICHAEL. Is that his name?

LAURA. Yes.

MICHAEL. Who is he?

LAURA. He's a friend.

MICHAEL. How do you know him?

LAURA. He's staying with me for a bit.

MICHAEL. I see.

LAURA. Not like that . . . He's just a friend.

MICHAEL. And he's a jack of all trades?

LAURA. No he's not. He's a carpenter. I'm sure there are masses of things he could turn his hand to but he is a carpenter. And he's unemployed at the moment. You're lucky to get him Michael.

8

MICHAEL. You speak from authority do you?

LAURA. What do you mean?

MICHAEL. He's been beavering away putting up shelves all over your flat has he?

LAURA. He's a good carpenter. I know he is.

Michael stops and looks towards the ceiling. He has just realised there is no sound coming from the attic.

MICHAEL. 'Doesn't sound like he's going at it hammer and tongs does it?

They are interrupted by the sound of Imogen's voice. She is approaching with Jonathan. She speaks very loudly. She shouts really.

IMOGEN. I must have my things in safe keeping Jonathan. You understand? Safe. By safe. They must be safe.

MICHAEL. What on earth . . . ?

ROANNA. Oh god.

Imogen and Jonathan enter. Imogen is weird looking. She is unkempt. She has ill assorted clothes. She is rather grubby. Her hair is dirty and matted.

Imogen comes into the centre of the room. Michael and Roanna and Laura stare at her. She avoids any contact with them.

IMOGEN. You said I could have these things safe. Away from them all. They want my things. I can't trust them. You see? I can't. There is nobody there who is to be trusted.

JONATHAN. They are safe.

IMOGEN. Where are my things? My things are stolen from me. Where are my boxes? Where are my boxes? Look here for my boxes. You said my boxes were here.

JONATHAN. Your boxes are here. They're okay. Okay?

Roanna holds the bin liner out towards Jonathan.

ROANNA. In here.

Jonathan takes the bag and takes the boxes out of it.

JONATHAN. See?

IMOGEN. I can't store them in my home. Because they won't have me. They threw me out. Of home. Out. They threw me out. What am I supposed to do? Just a poor little person out there on the boat with things needing somewhere on the shore. I know there are things. Will you listen? There are all these things which have to be put somewhere now. Are you ready for putting my things into safe storage? My family would have them from me. My family has taken almost all I have away from me.

ROANNA. We can't have these things in the house. . . . Anywhere.

JONATHAN. It might be best if . . . Why don't I . . . ?

He starts putting the boxes back into the bag.

Why don't I just put them in here and then . . .

IMOGEN. My sister took things. Now. Now. And then. And even. And knew. And knew and wouldn't say. And wanted my things. Always. Always. Through our child time. All the child time. She started with things and then went to men. I had menfolk. I did. I certainly did. And she took them from me. Did. Did. Did. She did. Take them from me. I want my men put upstairs in their boxes. But not . . .

JONATHAN. We'll find somewhere else to put them.

Imogen suddenly takes in the others. She addresses Michael.

IMOGEN. Have you been working? On a Saturday? Where? Where do you work on a Saturday? Why do you? That's not right. Why do you let them? They are out to steal from you you know? They are. Don't let them. Don't. It's not right. People want my things. They all do. I know they do. I have proof. Stealing. Stolen items. Proof.

PAUSE

MICHAEL. Can somebody tell me what's going on?

ROANNA. Jonathan's gone and . . .

IMOGEN. Why don't you answer? Tell me.

ROANNA. . . . put these boxes of Imogen's in the attic.

JONATHAN. You weren't meant to . . .

MICHAEL. What the hell for?

PAUSE

ROANNA. They've got to go *out*.

IMOGEN. They are all stealing from me now. Next door to my room. That man is trying to get into my room. He's drilling.

JONATHAN. No, that's Eddie Imogen. Eddie. He's putting up some shelves.

IMOGEN. I will have these men in their safety boxes upstairs. Will you listen to me. I need them . . . in their closed up space there. I want them there. She's drilling with him you see. They won't be safe. They won't be safe. Will you listen to me?

ROANNA. WE ARE LISTENING TO YOU.

PAUSE

JONATHAN. It's not your family next door Imogen.

IMOGEN. My family take things from me.

JONATHAN. But they're not next door are they?

IMOGEN. Drilling their way in.

ROANNA. That's Eddie: he's putting up shelves.

IMOGEN. Jonathan's a good boy. He listens to Imogen. No one else listens to Imogen. They should be locked up. My sister.

JONATHAN. Imogen . . .

IMOGEN. Locked up. And throw away the key. The bitch. Always stealing from me. I'm going to go round to see her and that puerile nancy boy playing with her privates down in the sandpit near Cleethorpes.

ROANNA. Christ!

MICHAEL. I've got to get out of this suit.

Michael begins to leave but is stopped by Roanna.

ROANNA. Please Michael.

Eddie appears at the top of the ladder and begins to climb down.

IMOGEN. And maybe hit her. She deserves it. There are things flying round you see. I know I've got to do it because they're telling me to. You see?

JONATHAN. How about if we take this stuff next door and hide it there?

IMOGEN. I will hit her because I can. I must. I want to. She deserves it. And they're telling me to.

JONATHAN. Who?

IMOGEN. Now. Telling me. Loud. I should have hit her then when she was coming up for air. But I missed it. I should have. Then. I've sworn I'll never do penance for a thing. Not evil like her. Not bad. Bad through and through and always stealing. More and more and more and my things and men.

ROANNA. *Will you stop it?* This is not appropriate behaviour.

SHORT PAUSE

I cannot have these things here. It's not convenient. You can see that it's not convenient. We're having things done in the attic. You can't barge in here demanding this, that and everything else. Can't you see people here are busy? You're not the only person here. You're not the only person who's got things to sort out. We all have.

PAUSE

Imogen takes the bin liner from Jonathan. She looks about her.

IMOGEN. I'm sorry to be disturbing your little party. I shall be throwing a party soon myself. You must come. Black tie. At six. We'll have a whale of a time.

Imogen begins to leave clutching her bin liner.

In about three weeks then? The weather should hold. Blue. Like today. And brilliant. Sun and true colour. We'll have to make do on the patio. But I'm sure we'll manage. I won't be inviting too many people.

She exits. Jonathan goes out with her.

MICHAEL. I see. A very trying morning.

ROANNA. I was hoping you wouldn't get back.

MICHAEL. I think you've seen her off alright: garbage and all. You must be Eddie?

LAURA. Yes, sorry. Eddie this is my brother Michael.

EDDIE. Hi.

MICHAEL. We seem to be a bit of a madhouse here I'm afraid. (They shake hands) Everything alright?

EDDIE. Well

MICHAEL. Good.

Jonathan enters.

ROANNA. Has she gone?

JONATHAN. Yes.

ROANNA. You saw her . . . leave?

JONATHAN. Yes.

PAUSE

Sorry: she followed me in. I told her I'd get . . . but she er . . .

ROANNA. I didn't know you'd even spoken to the woman.

JONATHAN. I've . . . said . . . 'hello' sometimes.

ROANNA. Why?

JONATHAN. 'Cos she says 'hello' to me.

ROANNA. You are a clot. Really.

JONATHAN. Chill out Mum. She's a bit . . . That's all.

ROANNA. A bit what?

JONATHAN. I don't know. A bit . . .

LAURA. There's no harm done Roanna.

ROANNA. I think I'm the best judge of that.

JONATHAN. She's taken it all away hasn't she?

LAURA. What was in the boxes?

JONATHAN. I dunno. But it was important. I had to put them somewhere.

ROANNA. Never never get involved with somebody like that. You don't know where it's going to end.

MICHAEL. Let's calm down shall we? She's gone.

JONATHAN. What could I do? I couldn't throw them away. I put them in the attic. She was happy. You weren't ever going to know.

ROANNA. I don't understand why you even speak to the woman.

JONATHAN. I can't ignore her if she comes up and talks to me.

12

ROANNA. Of course you can. From now on you'll give her a very wide berth.

JONATHAN. Okay, I made a mistake. A stupid mistake. What an opera. I don't see why it was actually but I'll take your word for it.

ROANNA. I'm sorry Jonathan but if she gets the encouragement she'll barge in here like that whenever she feels like it. None of you actually know what she's like. You're away. So are the girls. Michael's at work. It can be any time of the day or night.

MICHAEL. Now come on Roanna . . .

ROANNA. If only the place hadn't been turned into flats: she wouldn't be there.

MICHAEL. Sorry Eddie: we're involving you in a bit of a drama here.

ROANNA. I live in dread of it. She's completely unpredictable. You don't know what the boundaries are.

MICHAEL. What about a beer Eddie? You look like you could do with a break.

EDDIE. Yeah. Thanks very much.

MICHAEL. Where do you hail from?

ROANNA. I have to be in control of my own four walls.

EDDIE. Sorry?

LAURA. He means where do you come from?

ROANNA. I simply can't . . . Yes. A drink.

MICHAEL. It's coming! How are you getting on?

EDDIE. Well, er . . .

ROANNA. We could all do with a drink.

EDDIE. I'm hitting a few problems.

MICHAEL. Problems.

EDDIE. 'Fraid so.

MICHAEL. What sort of problems?

EDDIE. I may be wrong but I don't think so.

MICHAEL. What do you mean?

EDDIE. I . . . er . . . I think you've got some rot up there.

MICHAEL. Rot?

EDDIE. Yup.

ROANNA and MICHAEL (in unison). What sort of rot?

EDDIE. It's the bad one I'm afraid. I think you've got a patch of dry rot about . . . two feet, something like that . . . (he points to where it is) over there. It's on the party wall so it could be coming from them.

13

MICHAEL. What makes you think it's . . . ?

EDDIE. It's the smell. If you've ever smelt that smell you know it. And it's *that* smell. You can see it as well. It's early days . . . but there's a marbling. It's like . . . um . . . you know . . . It's not difficult to see. I didn't start off by it so it took me a bit to pick it up but . . .

MICHAEL. What does this mean?

EDDIE. Have it seen to. Now.

ROANNA. I don't believe it.

EDDIE. The good news is you'll be catching it early.

MICHAEL. That's something.

EDDIE. The bad news is I'll have to get all the wood out 'cos it spreads like wildfire.

ROANNA. I don't believe it. I live in a bouncy bloody castle.

BLACKOUT

SCENE TWO

Beside a road. Later the same day.

Eddie waits. Laura comes on in a state.

LAURA. What are you doing?

PAUSE

For God's sake Eddie.

EDDIE. I wanna talk.

LAURA. You can't jump out of the car like that!

EDDIE. You were at the lights.

LAURA. I know. But for God's sake.

EDDIE. I wanna talk.

LAURA. Why couldn't you talk in the car?

PAUSE

Look I'm really sorry today didn't work out better. I'm . . . mad about the attic. I thought you could do that for a couple of days, get in Roanna's good books and see what came of it. You know? I mean there's loads of stuff you could do about the place: odd jobs and things. I'm sure there is. Michael's loaded. It'd be no skin off his nose to give you a bit of help.

EDDIE. Why should he?

LAURA. Why shouldn't he?

PAUSE

EDDIE. So you want your brother to employ me doing odd jobs?

LAURA. I'm sure he will. I've just got to . . . I can always keep trying Roanna.

EDDIE. I've got to sort myself out.

LAURA. It would be a help though wouldn't it?

EDDIE. Yes // but . . .

LAURA. (interrupts) Every bit of money counts.

EDDIE. I know // but . . .

LAURA. Every hundred pounds is a hundred pounds you otherwise wouldn't have.

EDDIE. I need more than a couple of hundred quid.

LAURA. Of course you do.

EDDIE. What right have you got to put me down?

PAUSE

LAURA. What do you mean?

EDDIE. I don't need English translated for me: I speak English.

LAURA. What do you mean?

EDDIE. I know where I 'hail from'. I understand 'hail from'. You don't have to interpret for me. I can speak. I can answer questions. I didn't hear him. I didn't know he was talking to me.

LAURA. Oh Eddie I'm sorry. I'm terribly sorry. I don't know what I . . . I'm really sorry. I don't know what to say.

EDDIE. Are you ashamed of me?

LAURA. NO! No.

PAUSE

EDDIE. What *did* you tell Michael about me?

LAURA. I said you were a friend.

EDDIE. Is that all.

LAURA. I didn't want to go into it.

EDDIE. Why not?

LAURA. He wouldn't understand.

EDDIE. What's there to understand?

LAURA. Nothing. But he wouldn't. I know.

EDDIE. So I'm just a friend?

LAURA. Yes. Who's a carpenter. And who's out of work.

EDDIE. Who's also homeless and temporarily dossing in your flat.

LAURA. I did tell him you were staying.

EDDIE. But you didn't tell him why.

LAURA. He wouldn't understand.

EDDIE. He'd understand fine. He'd just refuse to believe it's real. That's what people do.

LAURA. So you think I should have told him?

EDDIE. I'm not ashamed of it.

LAURA. Of course not.

PAUSE

Sorry. I thought he'd see it as a label.

EDDIE. Your brother's alright.

LAURA. You think so?

EDDIE. He's got a beautiful fucking house.

LAURA. You didn't feel awkward?

EDDIE. When?

LAURA. In the house?

EDDIE. No.

LAURA. That's good.

EDDIE. I love posh houses. It's Disneyland. It's great.

LAURA. Michael did pay you didn't he?

EDDIE. For what?

LAURA. Doing all that in the loft.

EDDIE. Well I didn't . . .

LAURA. No, he's got to. It's not your fault his precious house is falling down. You were there for the day. So he's got to pay you.

Eddie puts his hands on Laura's shoulders.

EDDIE. Look Laura. Don't get yourself in knots about it. I've got to sort myself out.

PAUSE

Michael thinks I'm your boyfriend.

LAURA. He can think whatever he likes.

Eddie lets go of Laura's shoulders.

PAUSE

LAURA. What do you think somebody like me should do Eddie?

EDDIE. What about?

LAURA. About someone like you?

EDDIE. What do you mean?

LAURA. I'm just wondering if things are going wrong a bit.

EDDIE. Why?

LAURA. You've been at the flat . . . nearly three weeks isn't it?

EDDIE. Something like that.

LAURA. I keep feeling you're not . . . you know . . .

EDDIE. What?

LAURA. You don't seem to be doing very much about . . .

16

EDDIE. What?

LAURA. Well . . . Finding somewhere.

EDDIE. Give us a chance.

LAURA. I don't mean to . . .

PAUSE

EDDIE. I thought you liked me.

LAURA. I do like you.

EDDIE. Yeah?

LAURA. Of course I do. I don't dislike you. I don't know you. Is it helping you? Is there something else I should be doing?

EDDIE. Why should you do anything?

LAURA. Because I want to.

EDDIE. Great.

LAURA. I want to help.

EDDIE. Fine.

LAURA. I should.

SHORT PAUSE

EDDIE. Don't do it if you don't want to.

LAURA. No I do.

EDDIE. Good. 'Cos doing things you don't want to do is just dumb.

LAURA. What about things you have to do?

EDDIE. You never have to do things.

LAURA. What about responsibilities?

EDDIE. That's not the same thing. You've got to work out what you want to do and then do it. It's your choice. You've always got the choice.

LAURA. Eddie. Did you choose to get laid off after six weeks when you thought you were going to be working for three years? Did you choose to have your flatmate steal all your money and disappear to Tokyo? Did you choose to end up in a position where you couldn't afford to get yourself anywhere to live?

PAUSE

EDDIE. Look, do you want me to be in the flat or not?

LAURA. I don't mind you being there at all.

EDDIE. That's not the same thing: what do you want?

LAURA. What does what I want matter? That's got nothing to do with it.

EDDIE. 'Course it has. It's your flat. Do you *want* me there or not?

LAURA. How many times do I have to say it? You can stay there as long as you need to.

EDDIE. Do you *want* me to be there?

LAURA. I don't mind you being there at all.

EDDIE. Answer the fucking question.

LAURA. I don't know what I want. What does what I want matter?
We're all brought up on bloody want. What do you want for
Christmas? What do you want for your birthday? What do you want
for your wedding? What do you want for your divorce? What does
Dad want for his fiftieth? What does Mum want for mother's day?
Does Mum want to forget mother's day? Do you want to forget your
birthday? Do you want to forget thinking so hard and constantly
about what you want? *Things.* Do you want to stop having to want
fucking things and thinking that as long as you know what you want
so you know what you are after whether it's a navy and white,
sleeveless polo neck 100% cotton skinny rib sodding sweater or a
fucking partner who really wants you for who you are etcetera
etcetera, you'll be sorted out and sodding happy. Sod this sodding
want, want, want. It's all about greed.

PAUSE

EDDIE. There's not much point in having what you don't want because
that's not going to make you happy is it?

LAURA. Sorry. I *do* want you to be there. I've got the space. Stay.

EDDIE. Good.

LAURA. As long as it's helping.

EDDIE. Look Laura, if it wasn't for you I could be dead by now.

LAURA. Oh yeah?

EDDIE. You're my Guardian Angel.

LAURA. Shut up.

EDDIE. I'm serious. There are madmen out there. Barmy bastards
who've decided they don't like you. There was one in the hostel I
was in. . . . Pulled a knife on me. Big sodding army knife. There I
was having a bit of chat and suddenly there's this blade in front of
my face. And he's twisting it in the light so I get a good, proper
look.

PAUSE

I did the most brilliant thing I've ever done in my life. I offered him
a fag! I offered him a fucking fag. And he *smoked!* He was a
fucking smoker. They don't put that on fag packets do they? 'This
Could Save Your Life'.

Laura smiles.

You're cold.

LAURA. I'm alright.

EDDIE. You're shivering. You've got . . .

He picks something out of her hair.

LAURA. What?

18

EDDIE. It's gone.

LAURA. What was it?

He touches her hair.

EDDIE. You've got lovely hair.

LAURA. Have I?

EDDIE. First thing I noticed.

LAURA. Er . . .

EDDIE. That and your eyes. You've got intelligent eyes.

He moves away and laughs.

Don't worry: I'm not going to bite you.

LAURA. Shall we . . . ?

EDDIE. What?

LAURA. I *am* a bit cold. Let's . . .

EDDIE. You should smile more.

LAURA. Eddie . . . ?

EDDIE. Yes.

LAURA. What are you . . . ?

EDDIE. I don't know.

He puts his arm round her.

LAURA. Don't mess about do you?

EDDIE. No.

PAUSE

LAURA. Wow!

EDDIE. What?

LAURA. I don't know.

EDDIE. What?

LAURA. 'S a bit sudden.

EDDIE. Is it?

PAUSE

LAURA. I *knew* this was a risk.

EDDIE. I'm not threatening you.

LAURA. That's not what I mean.

EDDIE. What's the problem?

LAURA. When did you start thinking . . . ?

EDDIE. Day I moved in.

LAURA. Day you moved in?

EDDIE. Why not?

LAURA. I don't think we should.

EDDIE. Don't you?

LAURA. No. I'm sorry Eddie. I don't.

PAUSE

EDDIE. No. It was before I moved in.

LAURA. What was?

EDDIE. I started thinking.

LAURA. Was it?

EDDIE. You're an attractive lady.

PAUSE

LAURA. How do you know I don't want to be on my own at the moment?

EDDIE. Do you?

LAURA. There's nothing wrong with being single.

EDDIE. Isn't there?

LAURA. No.

EDDIE. What's right about it?

LAURA. I didn't want this to happen.

EDDIE. I think you did.

LAURA. Oh God.

EDDIE. Didn't you?

LAURA. *You* did.

EDDIE. Yeah I did. And I do.

LAURA. Oh God.

EDDIE. You're a tasty lady.

PAUSE

LAURA. Am I?

EDDIE. I started thinking . . . just a little bit of fantasy when // you were . . .

LAURA. (interrupts) This isn't a good idea.

EDDIE. . . . playing ping pong at the centre.

LAURA. I think we should . . .

EDDIE. . . . with Colin.

LAURA. Colin?

EDDIE. Yeah. Colin. From Newcastle. Colin in the little hat.

LAURA. Oh right. Colin.

EDDIE. What about you?

LAURA. What?

EDDIE. When did you start thinking?

PAUSE

LAURA. We don't have to do this.

EDDIE. No we don't.

EDDIE touches her cheek.

LAURA. If the centre knew I really would be in trouble.

EDDIE. So, they won't know.

LAURA. It's the only rule there is. They make it very, very clear when you go there and say you want to volunteer or whatever: No Involvement. Of any kind. I should never have offered to let you stay in my flat at all let alone . . . I'm really sticking my neck out having you there. That's why I'm not visiting the centre at the moment in case people start asking me . . . You know.

EDDIE. Well: you don't tell them: I won't tell them. It's not their business is it?

LAURA. Oh boy!

EDDIE. What?

LAURA. I know I shouldn't do this.

EDDIE. Sh.

He caresses her cheek.

LAURA. If you think about it it isn't that good an idea is it?

EDDIE. What about if you don't think about it?

LAURA. It may be alright for you but I know I shouldn't.

EDDIE. You should have what you want.

LAURA. There's a lot more to it than simply thinking about what you want.

EDDIE. Stop talking.

LAURA. What am I doing?

He kisses her.

EDDIE. Where's the car?

LAURA. Um . . .

EDDIE. We'll go somewhere quiet.

LAURA. In the car?

EDDIE. Yeah.

LAURA. What? You mean . . . in the car?

Eddie has started to explore under Laura's clothes.

EDDIE. Yeah.

LAURA. Um . . . I . . . um.

BLACKOUT

SCENE THREE

Setting: As in Scene One. Later the same day.

MICHAEL. He hasn't got the time to think about this now.

ROANNA. You have to plan ahead for these things like anything else.

MICHAEL. A year?

ROANNA. It's not a year. It's ten months.

MICHAEL. What's ten months?

ROANNA. It's ten months 'til the summer. If Jonathan wants to do one of these . . . go travelling . . . that's when it'll be.

PAUSE

I don't think we should just knock the idea Michael.

MICHAEL. Is it a good one?

ROANNA. I think we should give it a chance. Please let's not have // an argument

MICHAEL. (interrupts) An argument.

ROANNA. I don't want // him to . . .

MICHAEL. (interrupts) Nor do I.

PAUSE

ROANNA. This is the first weekend Jonathan's chosen to come home in three.

MICHAEL. He's got all his pals at school: it's not surprising. He should be boarding full time.

ROANNA. He isn't boarding full time: he's boarding weekly. And I'd like to see more of him. Okay? I don't want to spoil this weekend completely. I've already given him an earful about Imogen. Let's not have another one about this GAP business.

MICHAEL. What does it mean anyway? Building bridges in Nepal? Sailing to Papua New Guinea?

ROANNA. It's just an idea at the moment. I don't think we should squash it. I think at least he should go to the interview.

MICHAEL. I think he should get his head down.

PAUSE

ROANNA. It means taking a year off to be a volunteer and . . . go wherever they want to send you.

MICHAEL. Jonathan doesn't need a year off. He needs a year on. And what's a year? He shouldn't be thinking in years: he should be thinking in five years, ten. His future. He should be making the most of this last critical stage at school not whileing away the hours wondering about wandering around the world.

ROANNA. Oh I wish you two weren't at each other's throats all the time. It's so exhausting.

PAUSE

You don't give him any credit.

MICHAEL. I'd give him credit if there was anything to give him credit for.

ROANNA. There are masses of things Jonathan would be wonderful at. Will be. I know *exactly* what he should do. He should run a gallery. Or curator of a museum. Or go into antiques.

MICHAEL. He won't go into anything if he doesn't look out.

ROANNA. We've got to encourage him Michael. He's a sensitive boy, very caring . . .

MICHAEL. And stubborn. And bloody minded.

ROANNA. Oh for heaven's sake.

MICHAEL. You make him sound like the girls. He's a headstrong young man. He's 18. He's idealistic. He wants to do good. He's anti school because he's 18 so he's going to be anti something. He's anti me. I understand Jonathan very well. I'm amazed the school suggested this GAP business for a boy like him, who'll grab any excuse he can to get out of a bit of work. It's giving him the opportunity to put himself at the bottom. It's what the boys at the bottom do isn't it. Volunteering or globe-trotting. Grape picking. Labouring.

ROANNA. It wasn't the school's idea.

MICHAEL. Whose idea was it then?

ROANNA. Laura's.

MICHAEL. (exhales) Christ! . . . Christ.

BLACKOUT

SCENE FOUR

Laura's flat. A few hours on from the end of scene two.

After an hour or so in bed. Laura is in her dressing gown which is of the warm woolly variety. Eddie has thrown clothes on.

EDDIE. I love fucking middle-class girls.

LAURA. What?!

EDDIE. I love fucking middle-class girls.

LAURA. What do you mean?

EDDIE. They're sexy. You are. Very. Very, very sexy.

LAURA. Are we?

EDDIE. Yeah. Sexy and out of reach.

PAUSE

LAURA. Have you . . .

EDDIE. What?

LAURA. Nevermind.

EDDIE. And posh. Everything about you is good quality.

LAURA. But out of reach?

EDDIE. Middle-class girls aren't going to talk to me are they?

LAURA. So you haven't slept with dozens?

EDDIE. Me?

LAURA. It sounded like . . .

EDDIE. Oh yeah. Thousands. I've had thousands. Thousands of girls with those smiles. Teeth. Best quality everything. Well bred. Thoroughbreds. Fat chance. Middle class means you can look but don't touch.

LAURA. Not always. (She kisses him)

EDDIE. Why have you got a wedding ring on?

LAURA. Don't miss much do you?

EDDIE. You're not . . .

LAURA. No. I wear it for school. 'Are you married Miss'? 'Have you got a boyfriend'? 'Miss . . . What's your boyfriend's name Miss'? I got it every day til I dug this out of the drawer and . . . reinstated myself.

EDDIE. Go and stand over there.

LAURA. Why?

She goes and stands a little way from him.

EDDIE. I want to look at you.

She makes a move to sit down.

Stay where you are.

She stays.

You've got a lovely body.

LAURA. Have I?

EDDIE. I wouldn't say it if I didn't mean it.

PAUSE

You look great going off in the morning. I've been watching you and thinking . . .

LAURA. Yeah! Now I know what you've been thinking.

EDDIE. You look good.

LAURA. You have to. Kids don't miss a thing.

EDDIE. When are you going to get rid of that?

24

LAURA. (feeling her dressing gown) This?

EDDIE. Yeah.

LAURA. What's wrong with it?

EDDIE. It's horrible. Why haven't you got a nice slinky number so I can see your arse properly in it?

LAURA. Can I sit down now? Please sir?

EDDIE. Come on then.

She sits down.

EDDIE. Why haven't you got a telly?

LAURA. I did have one. It was stolen. 'S what comes of living on the ground floor.

EDDIE. I'll get another one.

PAUSE

Don't worry about it. You've got to relax.

LAURA. Some hope! 130 pupils a week. See the work. Mark it. Plus preparation. What time have I got to relax?

EDDIE. You've got now.

PAUSE

LAURA. So I should have a slinky number?

EDDIE. Treat yourself. It's Christmas. . . . We should go clubbing.

LAURA. Clubbing?

EDDIE. Dancing.

LAURA. I can't dance for toffee.

EDDIE. 'Course you can. With an arse like that you can dance great.

LAURA. I'm hopeless.

EDDIE. Everyone in the world can dance.

LAURA. I can't.

EDDIE. How long have you been on your own?

PAUSE

Eh?

LAURA. I don't want to tell you.

EDDIE. Why?

LAURA. It's a bit close.

Eddie laughs.

EDDIE. We've just had an hour in bed. Isn't that close?

LAURA. Yes.

EDDIE. So?

LAURA. I don't want to talk about it.

EDDIE. I don't want to talk about it I just want to know when you last slept with someone.

PAUSE

LAURA. A couple of years.

EDDIE. Years!!

LAURA. Yes.

EDDIE. Why?

LAURA. I don't know.

EDDIE. Years. Years. That's not right.

LAURA. I knew you'd think I was a freak: that's why I didn't want to say.

PAUSE

EDDIE. So you were married?

LAURA. Briefly.

EDDIE. What went wrong?

LAURA. What went wrong with yours?

EDDIE. You first.

LAURA. No you. Why should it be me?

EDDIE. She got demanding.

LAURA. Oh dear.

EDDIE. Wanting to know stuff. Wanting me to pick the kid up.

LAURA. The kid?

EDDIE. I've got a little girl.

LAURA. Have you?

Eddie nods.

EDDIE. I'll pick her up. I don't mind that. But she wanted . . . she wanted me to be there all the time. So she could get out and stuff. Just wanting me there. And I didn't want that. I can handle it if I'm not pushed. I can't be pushed. She's alright. She'll be with someone else by now. She wanted out as well.

LAURA. Did she?

EDDIE. Yeah. I'm not reliable.

LAURA. Aren't you?

EDDIE. I never pretend I'm going to be. I'll be there but only on my own terms. She knew that but she couldn't handle it. She got all demanding about it. She changed. That was it really. If she hadn't changed I'd still be there . . . I might be.

LAURA. Do you miss her?

EDDIE. Nah. She was a bit of a cunt really.

LAURA. Don't say that.

26

EDDIE. What?

LAURA. That word.

EDDIE. Cunt?

LAURA. Yes.

EDDIE. Why?

LAURA. What do you mean by it?

EDDIE. I hate her.

LAURA. Fine. Say that.

EDDIE. I had to come down here to get away from her.

PAUSE

LAURA. So you're a Dad?

EDDIE. Yeah. I've got two kids: boy and a girl.

LAURA. Two? You've got two children?

EDDIE. Yeah.

PAUSE

LAURA. Wow.

EDDIE. What?

LAURA. I didn't realise. Why didn't you say?

EDDIE. It's never come up.

LAURA. Don't you think you should . . . be with them?

EDDIE. No I fucking well don't. You don't know anything about it Laura. Okay? I love my kids but their mothers are both cunts . . . Sorry. I mean I don't like their mothers.

LAURA. Tell me about them.

EDDIE. Their mothers?

LAURA. The children.

EDDIE. My boy's twelve now, no, thirteen. And my little girl's three. My boy's got a new dad. His mum went and married him when he was . . . three, something like that. She's got other kids now. I don't see him. She doesn't want me to see him. I'm not going to let that happen with my little girl. She's gorgeous. She's the spit of me.

PAUSE

Why haven't you got kids?

LAURA. I got divorced.

EDDIE. So?

LAURA. There's never been anyone else . . . not to . . . you know.

EDDIE. What went wrong?

LAURA. It was a mistake.

EDDIE. Why?

LAURA. It didn't work.

EDDIE. Why didn't it work?

PAUSE

Eh?

LAURA. It just didn't.

EDDIE. Did he go off with someone?

LAURA. Yes. Okay. That's what went wrong. He went off with someone.

EDDIE. Bad luck.

LAURA. He never wanted to marry me. He married me because he thought he should.

EDDIE. Were you pregnant?

LAURA. No.

EDDIE. What then?

LAURA. He felt sorry for me. My parents died. We were going out with each other. We got married.

EDDIE. How long did it last?

LAURA. Long enough. Come on. (She holds out her hand for him.) What are we talking about this for? We were having fun. (Eddie takes her hand.) What colour dressing gown?

EDDIE. Any colour. But silk. Classy.

BLACKOUT

SCENE FIVE

The gates to Jonathan's school. Mid December. A weekday. Mid afternoon.

Imogen is standing by the gates. She is dressed in bright colours and holding a balloon.

Jonathan approaches. He is wearing school uniform. He is agitated. He glances about him. He checks that he isn't being followed.

He arrives at where she is standing. They stare at each other. Imogen giggles.

JONATHAN. What are you . . . ?

PAUSE

IMOGEN. He was a nice man.

JONATHAN. Who?

IMOGEN. The man who went and got you.

PAUSE

JONATHAN. What are you doing here?

28

IMOGEN. What's his name?

JONATHAN. What are you doing here Imogen?

IMOGEN. Don't you remember?

JONATHAN. What?

IMOGEN. His name?

JONATHAN. Mr Shepherd.

IMOGEN. Very nice.

PAUSE

JONATHAN. I can't come out. I'm not allowed to.

IMOGEN. Prison.

JONATHAN. What?

IMOGEN. Not allowed out.

JONATHAN. No it's not a prison. It's a school. It's school rules. I can't come out. Why have you come?

IMOGEN. They put me in prison sometimes. Not gates like these.

Imogen wanders towards the gates. Jonathan blocks her.

JONATHAN. You can't come in. I'm sorry Imogen. Do you want something?

Imogen hovers on the threshold.

IMOGEN. Is he one of your teachers?

JONATHAN. Yes. Biology. I'm not allowed visitors.

PAUSE

You can't come in.

Jonathan looks at his watch.

IMOGEN. It's Wednesday.

JONATHAN. I know it's Wednesday.

IMOGEN. Is it a nice school? Do you enjoy it? Are you enjoying your time here at the school? It is in a very nice location isn't it? I must say.

JONATHAN. Yes it is. It's fine. It's okay. It's . . . How did you know where to come to?

IMOGEN. On the train.

JONATHAN. I'm going to get shit for this.

PAUSE

IMOGEN. Jonathan?

JONATHAN. Look I . . .

IMOGEN. No you don't.

JONATHAN. What?

IMOGEN. Look.

PAUSE

IMOGEN. You're not looking.

JONATHAN. What are you talking about?

Jonathan looks back towards the school to see what she is talking about.

IMOGEN. You're not looking.

JONATHAN. At what?

IMOGEN. There's someone here to see you.

JONATHAN. Where? Who?

Jonathan looks round thinking someone is approaching.

IMOGEN. Who's got something to show you.

Imogen goes up close to him.

JONATHAN. Who?

IMOGEN. Here.

He looks at her. She nods.

JONATHAN. What Imogen? What do you mean?

Imogen walks off.

PAUSE

Look: we're not allowed visitors. Why didn't you tell me? Why didn't you say? I could have told you. I don't mind if you write me a letter Imogen but you *can't* come to the school. Now you've got the address you could write me a letter but you mustn't come. I'll answer a letter. I promise. I will. I don't mind. But you mustn't come.

PAUSE

I'm sorry. You'll be able to find your way back won't you? I mean you got here so you must have the ticket home. Did you come on the train?

IMOGEN. I came to see you.

JONATHAN. I know. *Why?*

SHORT PAUSE

Look Imogen: someone's going to come up any minute and I'm going to be in real trouble.

IMOGEN. To show you my hair.

PAUSE

JONATHAN. *What?*

IMOGEN. To show you my hair.

JONATHAN. What do you mean?

IMOGEN. I've had my hair done.

Jonathan realises that Imogen has had her hair done.

30

SHORT PAUSE

JONATHAN. Great.

IMOGEN. Do you like it?

JONATHAN. Umm . . .

IMOGEN. She said it changed me; I look better. I should have it done regularly. It makes a big difference. It makes you feel wonderful having your hair done. She said all that to me as she was doing it. I didn't look til she was finished and then I did.

JONATHAN. Yeah . . . Yeah. I've got to go okay? I've really got to go.

He turns and begins to leave.

IMOGEN. (calls) Jonathan?

JONATHAN. (pausing) Yeah?

IMOGEN. Do you like it?

JONATHAN. Yeah. It's great. It's fine. It's . . . fashionable. Nice. Okay?

He makes a dash for it. He stops because she shouts.

IMOGEN. (shouts) I BROUGHT YOU A CAKE.

He tears back to get it. He holds out his hands ready. She fumbles in her bag for it. She brings out a very basic, oblong shaped, packaged cake. He grabs it and runs off.

(shouts) SO YOU CAN EAT NICE THINGS YOU LIKE.

He has gone. She watches him as he disappears from view. She feels her hair.

THE LIGHTS FADE.

SCENE SIX

Setting: As in Scene One. A couple of days later.

Michael and Laura enter. Michael is studying a receipt.

LAURA. So it's good news?

MICHAEL. Touch wood.

LAURA. Great.

MICHAEL. And these are Eddie's expenses?

LAURA. Yes.

MICHAEL. Ninety-four pounds and fifty-six pence. Is that right?

LAURA. If that's what it says.

MICHAEL. Ninety-four pounds fifty-six. Plus VAT. No: that includes VAT.

LAURA. He's saved you a lot of money Michael.

MICHAEL. He hasn't saved me a penny. That's the point. He's saved Roy a lot of money.

LAURA. Because all the rot started on his side?

MICHAEL. That's right. Dear old Roy is going to have to foot the bill to hack off the plaster on our side, let alone what he's got to do on his, two whole meters up all along the party wall, plus 2 meters across of new floor, including joists, pretty much from front to back. (he gestures the extent) So, right from that corner, over our heads to the other side and over, floorwise, nearly to the hatch.

LAURA. Oh.

MICHAEL. Everything they found was above floor level or we'd . Roy'd . have had to go downstairs and . . . (he shakes his head)

LAURA. That would have cost more?

MICHAEL. It could have trebled it. I feel like the cat who got the cream.

LAURA. And you've got Eddie to thank for it.

MICHAEL. That it's not my responsibility?

LAURA. That he was up there working and discovered the problem.

MICHAEL. Absolutely. Ten out of ten to Eddie. He's a nice chap. How is he?

LAURA. Trying to get work.

MICHAEL. Of course. So what do I owe you?

LAURA. You owe Eddie that plus his fee.

MICHAEL. He didn't finish the job.

LAURA. He couldn't finish the job.

MICHAEL. So I've got ninety quid's worth of timber sitting outside in the garden for nothing.

LAURA. That's not Eddie's fault.

MICHAEL. Well I don't know . . .

LAURA. It isn't.

MICHAEL. He beavered away getting all the stuff up there in situ ready to go. And then he slaved away getting it all out again making a *Hell* of a mess in the process and . . .

LAURA. He *couldn't* finish the job. He put the hours in. He worked hard when he was here. You've got to pay him Michael. He was here from half past eight . . .

MICHAEL. Laura. Laura. Laura. I'm winding you up. Where's your sense of humour?

PAUSE

LAURA. I don't find that funny.

MICHAEL. That's put me in my place.

PAUSE

LAURA. Eddie could put some shelves up for you somewhere else with the wood that's sitting in the garden.

MICHAEL. I'm sure he could.

LAURA. He needs the work.

MICHAEL. I know he does.

LAURA. Badly.

MICHAEL. I hear you.

LAURA. He's a good carpenter. He's a craftsman.

MICHAEL. To my knowledge we are not in need of any new shelving at the moment apart from in the attic which, we both know is presently a no-go area. As soon as the situation alters I'll hot foot it to the old telephone and give you a buzz.

PAUSE

LAURA. You could put some shelves up over there.

MICHAEL. Where?

LAURA. There. You could put at least eight shelves on that wall. Well, maybe six.

MICHAEL. Where?

LAURA. From the door jambe straight across. You could have them moulded along the edge and each a couple of inches longer than the one above so they would descend to a long shelf at the bottom where you could arrange your nick nacks.

MICHAEL. That would look terrible.

LAURA. Now who's got no sense of humour?

MICHAEL. Okay! So I'm to make a cheque out to . . . ?

LAURA. Couldn't you give me cash?

MICHAEL. Why?

LAURA. I don't think he'd want a cheque. He needs cash.

MICHAEL. Why, doesn't he have a bank account?

LAURA. It's easier.

MICHAEL. Right. I'll make it out to you. And you can give him cash.

LAURA. Okay.

Enter Jonathan.

JONATHAN. Auntie L!

LAURA. Hello.

They embrace.

Still in one piece?

JONATHAN. Just about.

LAURA. What was it like?

JONATHAN. I'm never going to go to an interview ever again. It was terrifying.

Michael feels in his pockets to see if he's got his cheque-book on him. He has. He takes it out and writes out the cheque.

LAURA. Was it?

JONATHAN. There was a panel. Eight of them. Sitting along this big table. And me.

LAURA. God.

JONATHAN. They wanted to know how I bonded with people . . . how I'd manage on my own . . . what I was like in a team . . . What I had to offer. It was terrifying. I was in there over an hour.

LAURA. How do you think it went?

JONATHAN. Um . . .

MICHAEL. Come on Jonathan: it went fine.

JONATHAN. Hope so.

MICHAEL. 'Course it did. Um . . . didn't we make an arrangement . . . about work?

JONATHAN. Yeah.

MICHAEL. The weekend doesn't mean two days off.

JONATHAN. Dad . . . I need a break.

MICHAEL. We agreed you were going to do some work.

JONATHAN. I've been in my room for hours.

MICHAEL. Listening to music.

JONATHAN. I *have* been working.

    PAUSE

LAURA. How is school?

JONATHAN. Boring.

LAURA. It's only a couple of weeks to Christmas.

JONATHAN. Yeah. Brilliant. Can't wait.

MICHAEL. Jonathan's fibbing. School's been pretty dramatic recently hasn't it? Riveting.

LAURA. Oh?

MICHAEL. Jonathan had a visitor.

JONATHAN. Oh no Dad, don't.

MICHAEL. His pal Imogen turned up at the school gates.

LAURA. Really?

MICHAEL. Yes. Done up to the nines. Wasn't she? . . . with a balloon!

Jonathan nods.

LAURA. How did she know where you went to school?

Jonathan drops his head.

MICHAEL. Jonathan must have told her.

JONATHAN. I've never told her.

MICHAEL. She found out somehow. She was in her pink, blue, orange, lavender, green with a splash of lurex regalia.

JONATHAN. It wasn't that bad actually.

MICHAEL. With her balloon! Oh, to have been a fly on the wall.

LAURA. What happened?

JONATHAN. She arrived in a study period. Mr Shepherd came and got me. She didn't come in: she stayed at the gates.

MICHAEL. She wanted to though didn't she? She's taken a liking to our Jonathan.

JONATHAN. She hasn't.

LAURA. That must have been . . . very awkward.

JONATHAN. Yeah it was.

LAURA. At least nobody saw her.

JONATHAN. Yeah. But everybody knew. *Everybody.* It shot round the school like wildfire. 'Jonathan and his friend from the Funny Farm.' 'Jonathan's gone and got a dose of dementia. Better keep clear.' I'm going to be the butt of their jokes 'til I leave. I don't care though. It's their problem: if they can't handle it. They've got small brains. They've got no brains at all if all they can do is laugh. And snigger. Why should I worry? They're tossers.

MICHAEL. Thankyou.

JONATHAN. They are. You can't tie your tie wrong at school without everyone noticing. There's competitions on it. How to tie your tie. How big the knot is in your tie. That's the big issue at school. That and how you have your hands in your pockets. They're idiots. And they never let you off the hook about anything: let alone something as legendary as that.

MICHAEL. They'll forget it.

JONATHAN. They won't. I wish I wish I wish it had never happened. Not at school. If only it had been somewhere other than fucking school.

MICHAEL. That's enough of that thankyou.

JONATHAN. I feel so guilty. I couldn't think about anything other than me. Me. Me. Me. Me. Me. Me. If she'd been outside here . . . you know the way she wanders about . . . She'd have looked at me and said 'I've had my hair done' and I could have said 'That's nice' or something . . . But I couldn't do it there.

LAURA. Well, that sort of thing is really difficult.

JONATHAN. I was awful to her.

MICHAEL. She shouldn't have been there.

JONATHAN. I shouldn't have been like that to her.

LAURA. Like what?

JONATHAN. Beastly. She gave me a cake.

MICHAEL. Yummy. What flavour?

LAURA. Michael!

JONATHAN. I didn't even look at it. I threw it in a bushes. I smashed it up. I squashed it into the soil and pushed it in and covered it up and squashed it and . . . I shouldn't have done that.

MICHAEL. She shouldn't have been there.

JONATHAN. I should have // been able to . . .

LAURA. (interrupts) Jonathan: you mustn't feel bad about it.

A black bin liner, partly filled drops down out of the hatch onto the floor closely followed by another. Then Roanna starts to come down the ladder. She is dressed in old clothes to get grubby in. She is wearing a pair of rubber gloves.

ROANNA. That's it. There's nothing up there now. Nothing at all. They can just get on with it. Hello Laura. Michael showing you the good news?

LAURA. Yes.

ROANNA. (picking up the bin bags) I'm so looking forward to being shot of the whole thing. 'You having a break darling?

She exits with the bags not waiting for Jonathan's answer.

MICHAEL. Not any longer you aren't.

JONATHAN. I can't take any more in.

MICHAEL. Come on: enough's enough.

JONATHAN. I need a break.

MICHAEL. I'm not going to sit by and watch you fail. There's no reason whatever for you to not do bloody well in your 'A's. So get back into your room and get on with it.

JONATHAN. I'm doing my best.

MICHAEL. You're not doing your best by any stretch of the imagination. I've had a word with your housemaster and you're bone bloody idle. Your mother and I have not sacrificed what we have and struggled to put you through the best school, and the girls as well, for you to mess around and throw it down the drain. You tell me what kind of a future you think you're going to have if you cock it up now.

Jonathan starts to leave.

JONATHAN. See you Auntie L.

Laura just nods at him.

MICHAEL. Message received?

JONATHAN. Yeah yeah yeah.

Jonathan exits.

PAUSE

Michael tears the cheque out and gives it to Laura. She looks at it and gives it back.

LAURA. You haven't signed it.

Michael signs it.

LAURA. If that teacher was under me I'd do everything I could to get him sacked. You should never say that sort of thing to a child. You should never label a child as 'bone bloody idle'. Never.

MICHAEL. Jonathan's not a child.

LAURA. Alright. Pupil. Student. A teacher who says that sort of thing is a teacher who shouldn't be in teaching. The first . . . the first . . . thing . . . Teachers need to be people who *like* children. You're there to take care of them not // to bully them.

MICHAEL. (interrupts) He didn't say that.

LAURA. What do you mean?

PAUSE

MICHAEL. Jonathan and I have an understanding. He needs a rocket under him to get anywhere. I've got to push him. He knows that. He doesn't improve. So I push him harder.

LAURA. You mean his house master said nothing of the kind?

MICHAEL. His house master thinks he's bone idle.

LAURA. But he didn't say it?

MICHAEL. Don't interfere Laura.

LAURA. I'm not interfering.

MICHAEL. You're pretty close.

LAURA. I don't interfere.

MICHAEL. You don't interfere?

LAURA. No I don't.

MICHAEL. For someone who 'doesn't interfere' you've // got . . .

LAURA. (interrupts) Did you hear me just now when you were ranting at him?

MICHAEL. You've got too big an influence over him.

LAURA. I have?

MICHAEL. Yes you have.

LAURA. And I take it this 'influence' is negative . . . in your opinion?

MICHAEL. Yes it is.

LAURA. Thanks.

MICHAEL. Laura . . .

LAURA. I take the influence I have over children and young people with the utmost seriousness.

MICHAEL. I am not disputing that you are an excellent teacher.

LAURA. But you are telling me I'm bad for Jonathan. What the hell are you talking about?

MICHAEL. Jonathan isn't getting his head down and keeping it there. He'll take any distraction. This GAP year is music to his ears. An enticing way out of making some adult bloody decisions. The 'what am I going to do with myself' decisions.

LAURA. Maybe he's not ready to make those yet.

MICHAEL. And how's a year postponing it going to get him any closer?

LAURA. I don't know. I suppose it might not.

MICHAEL. Then why did you suggest it? At best it's a gamble and at worst it's a complete waste of time.

LAURA. I didn't suggest it.

MICHAEL. I thought . . .

LAURA. You thought wrong.

MICHAEL. So whose idea was it?

LAURA. It must have been Jonathan's.

MICHAEL. Who put it there?

LAURA. You'd better ask him.

PAUSE

MICHAEL. Is this cheque right now?

He gives her the cheque. She glances at it and then puts it away.

MICHAEL. I'm sorry: Roanna told me it was your idea.

LAURA. Surprise, surprise.

MICHAEL. No: I should apologise. I've accused you and . . .

LAURA. Of an excellent idea in my opinion. But it wasn't mine. This hasn't got anything to do with me. It hasn't got anything to do with this taking a year out after school either.

PAUSE

You don't like your own son. It's really painful to witness.

MICHAEL. That's . . . It's . . . ridiculous.

LAURA. It isn't. Look at the way you laugh at him. That incident at the school must have been awful for him.

PAUSE

You don't like him. He knows it. It's staring me in the face. Roanna probably loses sleep over it. Thanks for the cheque. I'll get the money to Eddie ASAP.

She exits.

BLACKOUT

SCENE SEVEN

Laura's flat. December 20th.

Laura is decorating the Christmas tree. Eddie enters. He has been out. He takes in the tree.

EDDIE. Looks nice.

Laura ignores him. He crosses over and comes up behind her and puts his arms round her waist. She moves away.

EDDIE. What's up?

LAURA. Nothing.

PAUSE

EDDIE. Something's up. What is it?

LAURA. I'm tired.

EDDIE. Give us a hug then.

LAURA. Not at the moment.

EDDIE. Why? Do I smell or something?

PAUSE

LAURA. What have you done today?

EDDIE. Look at me.

She does.

LAURA. What have you got round to doing today?

EDDIE. What's the matter?

LAURA. Nothing's the matter.

EDDIE. What are you saying?

LAURA. I'm not saying anything.

EDDIE. You're always saying something without saying it.

LAURA. I just asked what you've done today. It's a simple question. What have you got round to doing today?

EDDIE. What's the 'got round' bit mean?

LAURA. It doesn't mean anything. What have you done today? I've been to work. Seen the kids Christmas show. Spoken to eight, uptight, angry parents. Bought a Christmas tree on the way home. What have you done?

EDDIE. Good for you. Aren't you lucky?

LAURA. God's truth. You can't have sat around here all day. It doesn't matter what you've done but you must have done something. So what is it?

EDDIE. I've sat here. I've watched telly.

LAURA. All day?

EDDIE. All day.

LAURA. Fine.

EDDIE. Don't ask me what I do.

LAURA. Why?

EDDIE. 'Cos I don't like it.

LAURA. What have you got that's such a secret?

EDDIE. None of your fucking business.

PAUSE

Laura decorates the tree.

Yesterday I walked to The Elephant and Castle and . . . there was no work. And then I walked to Waterloo and . . . there was no work. And then I walked back here. Today I thought I'd sit on my arse. Which I have done all day apart from now when I went out and got some fags. Say What You Mean.

LAURA. It's very bloody difficult.

EDDIE. Why?

LAURA. Because I feel I shouldn't feel what I'm feeling.

EDDIE. Christ!

LAURA. I can't say anything because anything I say sounds bossy.

EDDIE. Come here.

She doesn't go to him.

Alright, I didn't go and see him about the job.

LAURA. I know. Why?

EDDIE. Don't try and tell me what to do.

LAURA. I'm not.

EDDIE. As long as you're not: that's okay.

LAURA. All I'm trying to do is make suggestions.

EDDIE. Why? Don't you think I might be the best judge of what I ought to be doing?

LAURA. I'm just trying to help.

EDDIE. If I don't want to do one of these little things that's 'helping' then I'm not going to do it. Right?

LAURA. Even if it is something which might really be helpful?

EDDIE. You're a stupid fucking cunt you know, you fucking are.

LAURA. Don't call me that.

EDDIE. What?

LAURA. You know.

EDDIE. Stupid?

LAURA. Cunt.

EDDIE. Well you are. And blind as well. I'm not going to work for eighty quid a week. Not for anybody. I'm not going to have any fucker exploit me on crap money like that. I worked for eighty quid a week when I was a kid. Now I work for three or four hundred. Why the fuck should I work for less? I'm a craftsman. I'm skilled. I'm a carpenter. I don't work evenings and nights for two quid an hour counting bottles of Sanatogen and Paracetamol on chemist's shelves. I'm skilled.

LAURA. I didn't mean it as a proper job: I thought it might help.

EDDIE. It doesn't help. It's stupid. I need proper money. I don't need ten P.

LAURA. You haven't got a job at all. Surely eighty pounds a week's a start.

EDDIE. How old do you think I am, eighteen?

LAURA. Where's the harm in it.

EDDIE. I'm telling you it's a shit idea. It's a shit idea. Right?

LAURA. If you say so.

EDDIE. I thought you wanted to help me out.

LAURA. I do.

EDDIE. So don't send me off to poxy little jobs which don't pay anything.

LAURA. Sorry.

EDDIE. What planet do you live on?

LAURA. I've said I'm sorry.

EDDIE. How much do you earn? It's not eighty quid a week is it? It's not nothing. Who can live on that? Who can keep going on it even? Maybe my mum was right: I should have stayed in the army and got paid to get myself killed.

LAURA. Point taken. I didn't think about it properly.

EDDIE. What's the difference between you and those ponses in Rolls Royces? 'Surely he can do something'? 'Sweep the streets. Anything'. 'Go down the sewers'. Eat Shit. Homelessness isn't the fucking problem. Money's the problem. And money comes from employment. No one wants to live on fucking benefits. You don't know about benefits though do you?

LAURA. I'm learning.

EDDIE. If I went for that job I'd lose my benefit.

LAURA. But you hardly get anything.

EDDIE. I'm not going to lose my entitlement so I can get exploited by some cunt.

PAUSE

LAURA. Okay: I'll tell you how I'm feeling. I'm feeling a complete

41

fool. A few weeks ago I was wandering around here thinking, 'I can help this person. All he needs is somewhere to stay'. Why can't I follow my convictions? Why are we all so full of doubt? Who am I to doubt this person I don't even know? And then I'd think, I don't even know him. What am I doing? It went round and round. Am I going to put my money where my mouth is and go out and do something for someone or am I going to make excuses so I don't have to get involved because I'm scared or . . . I don't know what. And then I looked round here and I thought, 'I could fit half the centre in bunk beds in here. What am I hesitating for'?

Everything's a leap of faith isn't it? Anything you ever do is. If you book a holiday you just do it. It could be great. It could be the poxiest waste of money you've ever made in your life. But you just do it. I wanted to *do* something. There are loads of people like me, loads who are sitting at home wondering why they aren't doing anything. And now I know. Because it's not simple. We're irritating each other. We don't understand each other. We don't know each other. We're not like each other. You don't want me to tell you what to do. You don't want me to ask you what you do do. So what am I supposed to do?

EDDIE. You haven't got to do anything. How can it be up to you? It's not your fault there isn't any real work.

PAUSE

There's no network out there: I just keep meeting people like me.

PAUSE

I'm trying. I know I can't stay here forever.

LAURA. It's not // that I want you to

EDDIE. (interrupts) No I know I can't.

LAURA. Let's just . . .

EDDIE. I don't want to get on your nerves.

LAURA. Sorry. I shouldn't have . . .

EDDIE. Come here.

She hesitates.

Come on. Please.

She goes over to him.

LAURA. I shouldn't expect . . .

He puts his arms round her.

EDDIE. I don't know where I'd be without you at the moment Laura. But I need a proper job: the real thing.

LAURA. Yes.

EDDIE. It's going to take time.

PAUSE

Sorry: I was a bit out of order. I know you mean well.

LAURA. Thanks.

Eddie kisses her.

EDDIE. You mustn't get all in a state about me. I don't like that.

PAUSE

Is it too much?

LAURA. What?

EDDIE. My being here?

LAURA. No.

EDDIE. Because . . .

LAURA. It's nice. Yeah . . . It's nice.

She looks at the Christmas tree.

Is that a bit over the top?

EDDIE. What?

LAURA. Having a tree? Just for us?

PAUSE

Is it?

PAUSE

Go on. Say.

PAUSE

EDDIE. No.

LAURA. Do you hate Christmas?

EDDIE. Um . . . No.

LAURA. You sound all hesitant.

EDDIE. Look . . . Um . . . I don't know that I'm going to . . .

LAURA. Come on. You've got to enter into the spirit of it haven't you? Otherwise it's depressing.

She hands him a decoration to put on the tree.

Bung that somewhere.

Eddie stands there turning the decoration in his hands.

THE LIGHTS FADE.

SCENE EIGHT

Laura's flat. Mid afternoon. December 23rd.

Laura lets herself into the flat being as quiet as she can. She has a couple of bags of shopping with her. She puts these down silently.

She takes her coat off. She takes a silk dressing gown out of one of the

43

bags and slips it on.

She calls softly.

LAURA. Eddie.

She kicks her shoes off and does a little twirl.

Eddie?

She stops. She calls:

Eddie?

She goes into the bedroom.

She comes out of the bedroom. She goes into the kitchen.

She comes out of the kitchen. She notices an envelope sitting in the top branches of the Christmas tree. She stares at it from where she is standing which is a distance from it.

She approaches the tree. She takes the envelope down. She stands holding it, looking at it, waiting to open it.

She opens it. A set of keys drops out of the envelope onto the floor. She picks the keys up. There is a Christmas card in the envelope. She takes it out. She opens it. She reads it.

PAUSE

She speaks to the card.

LAURA. Thanks. . . . Thanks loads Eddie. Tons . . . HAPPY BLOODY CHRISTMAS TO YOU TOO. All I want for Christmas is some crap like this, some crap like this, some crap like this.

She takes the dressing gown off and folds it up carefully. She returns the folded kimono to its bag.

BLACKOUT

INTERVAL

SCENE NINE

A room in The Homeless Person's Day Centre. December 28th.

Laura is sitting waiting.

Christine, Director of the Centre, comes in and sits down.

CHRISTINE. I'm very sorry this has happened Laura.

> PAUSE

> It isn't the first time something like this has . . . It's always difficult to . . . handle.

LAURA. How did you know?

CHRISTINE. It's our business to know. Eddie was, maybe is a client of ours. And we haven't seen *you* for a while have we?

LAURA. No.

CHRISTINE. So . . .

> PAUSE

> And men brag I'm afraid.

LAURA. He didn't . . .

CHRISTINE. No. Not in a particularly noisy way but a bit. He has friends here. I'm sorry you're . . .

LAURA. It's alright.

CHRISTINE. We would have known anyway. It's up to us to keep checks on people. That is our job. If Eddie was here one day and not the next he had to be somewhere. I don't like having to do this Laura. It's . . . These are things I *have* to say.

LAURA. Yes.

CHRISTINE. We have to protect our clients . . . from being led up the garden path.

LAURA. I didn't do that. Not at all. I thought I could help him.

CHRISTINE. People here need a great deal more than a sympathetic ear.

LAURA. I know that.

CHRISTINE. That can be a support; but it doesn't solve anything.

LAURA. It's water under the bridge now isn't it? Eddie just upped and left.

CHRISTINE. Of course he did.

> PAUSE

45

I take it he's back up north?

LAURA. I suppose so.

CHRISTINE. Then you don't know if he's got himself sorted out?

LAURA. No.

PAUSE

I thought it would be . . .

CHRISTINE. Relatively easy? Relatively straightforward? All he needs is da da, da da, da da, da da, da da and he'll be fine.

LAURA. Something like that.

CHRISTINE. Do you know anybody whose circumstances are straightforward?

LAURA. No.

CHRISTINE. Anybody whose life is clear?

LAURA. No.

CHRISTINE. Is yours?

LAURA. God no.

CHRISTINE. Then why on earth did you assume his was?

PAUSE

He just took you for a ride.

LAURA. No he didn't. I went into it with my eyes open. It's nobody's fault. Nobody did anything wrong. Apart from . . . I just wish it hadn't happened.

CHRISTINE. Did he steal things?

LAURA. No.

CHRISTINE. Cause any damage?

LAURA. No. He just left.

CHRISTINE. Then you were lucky. And . . . to be brutally honest with you . . . you got off better than you deserve.

PAUSE

We don't make these warnings casually. It's in everybody's best interest to be totally professional. No involvement of any kind. You knew that. You were told.

LAURA. And I learnt my lesson: I got hurt.

CHRISTINE. Well . . . Eddie's an attractive man.

LAURA. Yes.

CHRISTINE. Whereas Colin Bassett . . . Wingey whining Roger . . . Most of them here . . . aren't. Are they?

LAURA. No.

CHRISTINE. Who's rushing along to give them a helping hand?

PAUSE

Nobody is. Absolutely *nobody*. You picked the best of the bunch.

LAURA. I did think I could help Eddie.

CHRISTINE. Look: Eddie will survive. He's a Ducker and Diver. He'll get by. He's not asthmatic. He's not disabled. He's not too old to get another job. He's not alcoholic. Yet. He has no criminal record: as far as I know.

LAURA. But he does need help.

CHRISTINE. Of course he does. There isn't anyone here Laura who is shamming. Would you pretend to be homeless and stay in a dormitory with people who could turn out to be dangerous. for fun? Of course he needs help. Help in the form of cash. That's what would sort the Eddies out. So they can sort themselves out.

LAURA. Cash.

CHRISTINE. Cash. A job.

LAURA. I couldn't have given him a job. I tried to . . .

CHRISTINE. And you couldn't have given him money.

LAURA. Not really. I don't earn . . .

CHRISTINE. You're not 'the wealthy' are you?

LAURA. No.

CHRISTINE. You're just the 'concerned'.

LAURA. So what do we do?

CHRISTINE. Change society. Public disinterest and material wellbeing go hand in hand. The pursuit of material wellbeing breeds public disinterest. Educate people. Laura . . . I can't drag this out. This is is not something I like having to do but we are going to have to ask you to stop being a volunteer. 'Involvement' is something we can't . . . allow basically. We cannot be responsible for the consequences. I'm sorry. I'm afraid I have no choice.

BLACKOUT

SCENE TEN

Laura's flat. Two A.M. on the night of December 28th.

There is a persistent buzzing on Laura's intercom. After a little while Laura crosses the acting area going from her bedroom to the front door. She does her dressing gown (the old one) up as she goes. She passes a pile of stuff on the floor: rucksack, jacket, pair of shoes.

She gets to the door and hesitates. Then she presses the button.

LAURA. Hello?

We cannot really hear the answer. Laura does hear it. She moves away from the door. She tenses.

The buzzer goes again. She presses the button again.

LAURA. What?

This time we hear the voice more clearly.

EDDIE (OFF). Laura . . . Come on Laura, please. . . . Laura.

LAURA. What do you want?

EDDIE (OFF). Let us in Laura . . . Go on.

Laura moves away from the intercom working out what to do.

The buzzer goes again. She grabs it.

LAURA. Alright Eddie. I do know you're there. I'm thinking.

EDDIE (OFF) (muffled). Please.

She presses to let him in. She moves away from the intercom doing her
    dressing gown up tightly.

She opens the door. Eddie comes in. He is carrying a bag and bed roll.
    Laura shuts the door.

Eddie looks bad: markedly worse than in the previous scenes. He has
    been drinking. But he is compos mentis.

They stare at each other.

LAURA. You look awful.

EDDIE. She gave me an hour. I got one fucking hour. Christmas Day.
    Early. 'Before things get going.' One hour. Sixty minutes to the
    second. And then she was shot of me. (he breaks down) I got one
    hour with my little girl to see her open her present and then I was
    out on the street. And she can do that to me. I love my little girl. I'm
    a human being. I love her. One hour. She timed it. Out in the
    kitchen. Smoking. Watching the clock. Came in at the end and stood
    holding the door open with her bum. Rosie was crying. 'Plenty more
    presents and grandma and grandpa are over later and there's toys
    and presents and cake and games' and I'm out in the road. I couldn't
    see it. Couldn't see. Crying. She loves me. Her little arm round her
    present. And that cunt's going to change it. Change my present for
    something else. Just so it can't make her think of me. Rosie won't
    have anything of me. Like I don't exist.

Laura is ineffectual: she makes a stab at comforting Eddie who sobs.

LAURA. Why didn't you say you were going home?

Eddie breaks off.

EDDIE. What do you mean 'Home'? I haven't got a fucking home.

LAURA. No I mean . . . back. Going back.

EDDIE. I haven't got a fucking home. Remember?

LAURA. I know. Yes. Sorry. I . . .

   PAUSE

EDDIE. I couldn't even go to my Mum and Dad. I didn't have a present
    for them.

LAURA. Where have you been?

EDDIE. Out. I don't know. I thought I could get somewhere up there
but . . . That's what I was planning to do.

PAUSE

He sits down.

But I didn't . . . I had a job there . . . I had a home there.

PAUSE

I'm stuck. I can't even go back. I'm stuck . . . I'm one of them. I'm
stuck.

He spots the pile of things on the floor. He stares at it. An absolutely
still moment before he jumps up in a fury.

You cunt! Who have you got this time? Colin? Frank? You don't
muck about do you?

LAURA. What do you mean?

EDDIE. It can't be Malcolm. Malcolm stinks too much doesn't he?

LAURA. Eddie?

EDDIE. You cunt.

LAURA. What?

EDDIE. Still pulling with your moth-eaten dressing gown.

LAURA. What are you on about?

EDDIE. 'Helping' someone else now are you? I wasn't around at
Christmas so you went and got a replacement.

LAURA. Are you crazy?

EDDIE. Why did you want me to stay here? *Me* to stay here. And why
do you want 'him' now? (towards the bedroom)

LAURA. Eddie, you're wrong. You're mad.

EDDIE. We're just experiments for you. And your charity. You don't
want me to stay here. Me. A person. You never wanted to know
anything about me. A person with a life. You wanted a problem here.
That you could solve. So you could feel like Florence Fucking
Nightingale.

He is on his way out.

And you wanted a fuck. Fucking women. You're all cunts. You
want it. You don't want it. You want me. You don't want me.
You're cunts.

He exits. Laura stares at the open door.

PAUSE

The main door (onto the street) slams. Laura closes the door to the flat.

Jonathan comes out of the spare room. He is wearing his pyjamas.
Laura stares at the stuff on the floor.

JONATHAN. What's happening?

LAURA. Nothing.

JONATHAN. Auntie L.?

LAURA. Clear this stuff up will you?

JONATHAN. Auntie L.?

LAURA. Nothing's happening.

She goes into the bedroom and shuts the door. Jonathan starts picking the stuff up. The lights fade.

BLACKOUT

SCENE ELEVEN

Michael and Roanna's home: the same setting as in scene one. Two A.M. on the night of December 28th.

Heavy liturgical music is emanating from Imogen's flat next door. It is loud. Roanna is in her dressing gown. She has her ear against the wall.

Michael is beside her: also in his dressing gown.

ROANNA. Here. Right here. Where my ear is now. I'm right on top of it. She's got it jammed up against the wall. Exactly on this spot. The other side of the wall from here she's got speakers big enough to fill Wembley bloody Stadium. How far away is that? How thick's a wall? Six inches? Eight inches? Six. (she opens out her hand) What's that? Eight inches? An octave. It's an octave away. *One* layer of bricks. It's a common or garden party wall. It's not a fortress. One layer of bricks. A smear of plaster on either side of those. A couple of layers of wallpaper on that. And that's it. I'm separated from this dirge by wallpaper. I might as well move in with her. I might as well get into my nightie every night, grab a pile of records, go round and settle down to a night disturbing the whole neighbourhood at a thousand decibels all chumsy-wumsy with her. We could choose the repertoire together. We've got some good noisy stuff haven't we? A couple of oratorios. Massed choirs. Hundred piece orchestras. All those choral Last Symphonies. They'd liven it up a bit wouldn't they?

The music abruptly stops.

PAUSE

Michael and Roanna stand immobile.

I can't cope with it.

MICHAEL. How about a whisky?

ROANNA. She could be there for years. I could be standing here every night for the next ten years. Sleep deprivation is a known form of torture isn't it? That's what I'm going to say. That's going to be my new tack. 'Added to which I'd like to draw your attention to the long term health problems that the residents of Fitzroy Road are, without any shadow of doubt going to have to face in the future.'

She makes a move to go downstairs. Michael stops her.

MICHAEL. What are you doing?

ROANNA. I'm going to write it down. It's the only thing I can do. A dozen copies. To // anybody I can think of

MICHAEL. (interrupts) Not now. Do it in the morning when you've calmed down.

ROANNA. I can't calm down.

MICHAEL. Stop it.

ROANNA. I can't.

MICHAEL. You can. Just quieten down. You've let yourself get hysterical.

ROANNA. It's chaos. Rot on one side. A bloody lunatic on the other. It's driving me berserk.

MICHAEL. Roy is seeing to the problem of the rot. It's his responsibility and he's having it done. We've got nothing to worry about.

ROANNA. I'd like to see anyone cope with this better than me. *Anyone.* Night after night after night.

MICHAEL. She's only done this a couple of times.

ROANNA. Oh don't be so bloody reasonable.

MICHAEL. Someone's been in there and stopped her.

ROANNA. I can't believe she's back. *Already.* Every time she's taken in I think 'That's it'! And it never is. At least Jonathan isn't here. // She isn't keeping him up the whole

MICHAEL. (interrupts) What do you mean?

ROANNA. She isn't keeping him up as well.

MICHAEL. Why not?

ROANNA. He isn't here.

MICHAEL. Where is he?

ROANNA. Oh Michael!

MICHAEL. Where is he?

ROANNA. He's staying with Laura.

PAUSE

Had you forgotten?

MICHAEL. No I hadn't forgotten. Jonathan didn't tell me.

ROANNA. But you knew he was going to stay with Laura?

MICHAEL. I didn't know he was going today. I thought he was . . . I thought . . .

ROANNA. He's staying with Laura for a couple of days and we're going to meet up with them at the theatre.

MICHAEL. And I'm the last to know.

ROANNA. You aren't. I'm sure . . .

MICHAEL. I am. Why doesn't he talk to me: tell me what he's doing?

ROANNA. I'm sure he didn't mean to . . .

MICHAEL. Yes he did.

ROANNA. It's a mistake.

MICHAEL. Why doesn't he talk to me?

ROANNA. I don't know.

MICHAEL. I bet he's talking to Laura. 'Auntie L'.

ROANNA. It doesn't mean anything.

MICHAEL. Yes it does. I'm Public Enemy Number One with my own son.

ROANNA. You knew he was going to visit Laura.

MICHAEL. I don't know how I can get it right with that boy. I want to communicate with him. I'm trying. It's Christmas. It's the holidays. We've got time. And he buggers off to stay with Laura.

RANNA   You knew // he was going to

MICHAEL. (interrupts) Yes. I know. I know.

BLACKOUT

SCENE TWELVE

Laura's flat. 11.30 p.m. December 29th.

The room is empty. Laura has gone out.

Sound off of window breaking. Moments pass then Eddie stumbles on. He is drunk. He is in a belligerent mood. He looks about him. He goes off. He walks into something in the darkness.

EDDIE (OFF). Fuck.

He turns the light on. He knocks something over: sound of crockery breaking.

EDDIE (OFF). Fuck.

He comes on with a bottle of whisky about a quarter full. He drinks from it. He sets about looking for something. He shoves things about in his endeavour. Not finding what he is looking for he goes off.

***

Laura lets herself into the flat. She is followed by Roanna, Jonathan and Michael. They are all dressed up having just been to the show Laura was treating them to for Christmas.

ROANNA. I thought he was tremendous: I really did. It's a name to watch. You remembered the programmes Michael didn't you?

JONATHAN. I did.

Laura stops as soon as she is in the room seeing the furniture in disarray and the light on.

ROANNA. It was Peter something.

Eddie enters.

EDDIE. Haven't got much to drink over Christmas have you? You out of everything? Or are you not a drinker? Not much of a drinker. Moderation. All in moderation. Quite right.

PAUSE

You all been somewhere?

LAURA. We've been to the theatre.

ROANNA. Our Christmas present from Laura.

EDDIE. What d'you see?

LAURA. A show.

EDDIE. That's nice.

LAURA. It was.

EDDIE. Did you have a ticket for me?

PAUSE

No?

PAUSE

She's ashamed of me.

LAURA. You weren't here.

EDDIE. I used to be. When d'you buy the tickets?

PAUSE

LAURA. I didn't think you'd like it.

EDDIE. You didn't want me there.

LAURA. You wouldn't have liked it.

EDDIE. Why are they looking so surprised? We fuck. Didn't you know?

PAUSE

Don't think I haven't got a right to be here. I've got a right to be here. We fuck. That gives me the right doesn't it? You fuck her don't you?

LAURA. I'm sorry Michael . . .

EDDIE. Doesn't he?

LAURA. How did you get in? You haven't got your key Eddie. I know. You left it here. Remember?

EDDIE. Why's it got to be a secret?

LAURA. How did you get in?

EDDIE. Who are you to be ashamed of me?

LAURA. You broke in. Didn't you?

ROANNA. Oh God! Laura is . . . ?

EDDIE. You were out.

LAURA. You could have come back.

MICHAEL. Has he . . . ?

LAURA. It's alright: I know what he's done.

EDDIE. Let's put the cunt back in Scunthorpe.

MICHAEL. Shall I . . . ?

LAURA. No Michael I'll . . .

EDDIE. You showed me how. 'Remember'?

MICHAEL. I'll take that bottle.

EDDIE. You fucking won't. I haven't finished.

LAURA. What do you want Eddie?

EDDIE. Don't fucking want you. Don't want you now. Now I know what you're like. She'll fuck anything you know. She will.

LAURA. Do you remember Jonathan? Do you? Jonathan? Here? Do you?

EDDIE. Why?

LAURA. I'm hardly going to be having an affair with Jonathan am I? *He's* the person who's staying here. Okay? My own nephew.

PAUSE

Right?

EDDIE. You're still a cunt.

LAURA. Why have you come back?

EDDIE. You are. There's . . . There's . . .

LAURA. What?

EDDIE. Her whole life's about not being able to get a fuck: she's making a profession out of it.

LAURA. I'm sorry. He doesn't know what he's saying.

EDDIE. I do know.

LAURA. You're drunk.

EDDIE. You're frustrated.

LAURA. It's not a crime.

MICHAEL. And you're in a hell of a mess. You realise you've committed an offence breaking in here.

EDDIE. She told me what to do.

54

MICHAEL. Did you?

LAURA. No.

EDDIE. Liar.

LAURA. I told you I'd been burgled.

EDDIE. You showed me how.

MICHAEL. You've still broken in and it is still an offence.

EDDIE. What's it to you fuck face?

MICHAEL. I'm making you aware of the gravity of the situation.

EDDIE. She's desperate. She's had two years with her legs crossed. She's got lots of catching up to do.

ROANNA. Do you think we should . . . ?

EDDIE. She has. Probably more. Probably more like twenty. She can't get enough.

LAURA. What do you want Eddie?

EDDIE. What did *you* want?

ROANNA. Shall we call the police?

Laura shakes her head.

EDDIE. She says she wants to help people. She doesn't want to help people: she wants to . . . She wanted to help me but . . .

ROANNA. I think we should go and wait in the car. Jonathan why don't you go and collect your things?

JONATHAN. It doesn't matter Mum. It's okay. I understand what's going on: I'm not a child.

ROANNA. I want you to collect your things.

Jonathan goes off to do that.

EDDIE. You're one and all.

ROANNA. I beg your pardon?

EDDIE. You want to control people. That's what she wants. She wants to control people ς . . she wants them to be different. She wants to 'help' . . . and them to like her for it. But she doesn't. She wants them . . . She thinks she's good. She thinks she's helping . . . that makes her good.

LAURA. I don't.

EDDIE. Telling people what to do. How they should be.

LAURA. Please Eddie.

EDDIE. You want to sort yourself out. Who are you to be telling people . . . ? She said she wanted to help me.

LAURA. I did.

EDDIE. If I fucked you?

LAURA. What are you trying to prove?

EDDIE. Do you want to go to bed now?

PAUSE

Get a quick one in? Do you?

LAURA. No.

EDDIE. She's gone off me now. That's a shame. My wife's gone off me too.

MICHAEL. Your wife?

LAURA. He didn't tell me he was married.

EDDIE. You didn't tell me you were a frustrated fuck.

Jonathan comes in.

JONATHAN. Where do you keep your dustpan and brush?

LAURA. What?

JONATHAN. Where do you keep your dustpan and brush?

LAURA. Under the sink. Why? What's it matter?

JONATHAN. Sorry. It doesn't. I thought I'd . . .

ROANNA. What do you want it for?

JONATHAN. I thought I'd clear up the glass in the bathroom. He's smashed the window.

LAURA. I know he has. That's how he got in.

JONATHAN. Shall I . . . ?

LAURA. Yes. Go ahead. I don't care.

Jonathan goes off.

EDDIE. You didn't want to help me. You wanted a fuck over Christmas.

LAURA. Stop doing this Eddie. Please.

EDDIE. Didn't you?

PAUSE

It's all middle-class wank. Do something for some poor sod like me. Feel good about yourself. Congratulate yourself. And get a fuck into the bargain.

MICHAEL. Laura do you want me to . . . ?

EDDIE. Throw me out. Eject me from the premises.

LAURA. I wanted to help you Eddie. You know I did.

EDDIE. How?

LAURA. I didn't know how. I failed. But I tried.

MICHAEL. I think I should . . .

EDDIE. Call the police. Go on. Call the police. You want to.

LAURA. No. Don't do that.

MICHAEL. I think . . . This is quite ridiculous.

56

LAURA. Don't do it. I don't want that.

EDDIE. What do you want?

LAURA. I want you to go.

EDDIE. You're not going to ask me back?

LAURA. To stay here?

EDDIE. Yeah.

LAURA. There's not much point is there?

EDDIE. So that's the end of your charity?

LAURA. You didn't want it. You left. No warning. Nothing. Just a horrible little Christmas card. 'Too much to explain. Sorry. Bye bye. Eddie.' How do you think I felt?

EDDIE. I had to.

LAURA. No you didn't. Not like that you didn't.

EDDIE. I'm not sorry for you.

MICHAEL. What exactly do you want Eddie? Now?

PAUSE

EDDIE. I want my television.

MICHAEL. Your television?

EDDIE. Yeah. I want my television.

MICHAEL. Does he have a television here?

EDDIE. Yeah. You fuck. I have.

MICHAEL. Right. Where's his television?

LAURA. I'll get it.

ROANNA. I'll help you.

Laura and Roanna go off to get it.

MICHAEL. Where are you staying at the moment?

EDDIE. What's it to you?

MICHAEL. Absolutely nothing. I was simply asking.

EDDIE. You got a spare room?

MICHAEL. No.

EDDIE. I'm not staying anywhere. I haven't got anywhere to stay. My wife won't let me in. She won't let me see my kid. She won't . . . She won't . . . She . . . There's no job. I've no job. I've no home. I can't . . . I can't . . . I've no job. Laura said you wouldn't understand. I said what's there to understand? She said you wouldn't. But what's difficult about it? I haven't got a job. I haven't got a home. What's difficult about it?

MICHAEL. Why haven't you got a job?

EDDIE. Oh fuck off.

Laura and Roanna come on with the television.

LAURA. Here.

MICHAEL. I'll take it.

EDDIE. It's mine.

MICHAEL. I know it's yours.

He takes it.

> I'll hold it while you . . .

LAURA. Give me the bottle.

EDDIE. I haven't finished.

LAURA. Give it here. I'll give it back.

He gives her the bottle.

MICHAEL. Ready?

He tries to give Eddie the television. Eddie is too drunk to hold it. He nearly drops it. Michael sees this coming and grabs it back.

LAURA. Where are you going to put it?

> PAUSE

> Put it down Michael. He hasn't got anywhere to put it.

MICHAEL. Haven't you?

EDDIE. I told you I haven't got a fucking home. Have I? Laura?

Michael puts the television down.

Enter Jonathan.

JONATHAN. Have you got some card or something to put over the window? Or . . . bit of plastic or something.

LAURA. Oh I don't know.

JONATHAN. Okay. I'll have a look.

Jonathan goes off.

> PAUSE

EDDIE. I made a mess . . . Sorry.

LAURA. Doesn't matter.

> PAUSE

EDDIE. Can I stay?

> PAUSE

LAURA. I don't think so.

> PAUSE

EDDIE. Please.

LAURA. What for?

> PAUSE

EDDIE. Please.

58

LAURA. I don't want you to.

Eddie attempts to pick up the television. He can't do it.

EDDIE. You cunt . . . You cunt . . . I'm not going to let you have my television . . . You're not going to . . . Mine . . . I want . . . I'll . . .

Laura and Michael watch as he grapples with it hopelessly.

MICHAEL. How much did you pay for it?

PAUSE

How much did he pay for it?

LAURA. I don't know.

EDDIE. Thirty quid.

MICHAEL. I'll buy it off you.

EDDIE. Let me stay.

LAURA. I can't Eddie.

EDDIE. You can.

LAURA. It won't help.

Michael takes money out of his wallet and hands it to Eddie who takes it.

MICHAEL. Here. That covers it. You've even made a bit of profit.

Eddie takes the bottle from Laura.

EDDIE. You've got a beautiful house. I had a nice place. I had a nice place twice. You don't think it's going to happen to you. But it can. Can happen to anybody. That's the truth.

He starts to leave.

LAURA. Eddie I'll . . .

EDDIE. Bullshit.

He exits.

SILENCE

LAURA. Aren't we being British? Nobody's saying anything.

ROANNA. I'm sorry Laura. That was . . . really.

MICHAEL. But why on earth? . . . I mean . . . a chap like Eddie?

LAURA. When was the last time you were on your own at Christmas Michael?

PAUSE

Have you *ever* been on your own at Christmas?

MICHAEL. No. I suppose I haven't.

LAURA. So you don't know what it is like.

MICHAEL. You're always welcome to spend it with us.

LAURA. I always do and I'm always on my own.

PAUSE

MICHAEL. *Shall* I call the police?

LAURA. I think I've had enough humiliation for one day.

MICHAEL. You should report it.

LAURA. 'A friend of mine broke into my flat and tried to steal his own television.' I'd look as stupid as I feel.

MICHAEL. But . . .

ROANNA. Michael.

LAURA. It's quite an achievement isn't it: to get to your thirties and still not be able to say what you . . . want?

ROANNA. You don't have to say anything Laura.

LAURA. I wish you hadn't all been here. I'd have come home and found him being drunk and vile and staggering about and I'd have got rid of him myself. I'd have got up tomorrow and looked fine as if nothing had happened. And nothing would have happened because nobody would have known.

MICHAEL. He could have turned nasty.

ROANNA. He did turn nasty.

LAURA. I'd have done what millions of people do all the time: I'd have had a grubby little affair. In secret.

PAUSE

Do they feel ashamed? People have affairs don't they? They have daft affairs. They have the most crazy, unlikely, 'bound to end in disaster' flings. People get married and divorced and married again by the time it takes me to . . . The world is full of people like me. I get up and go to work. I *do* the work. Properly. Responsibly. And nothing ever happens. And when I do what other people do all the time I get beaten up . . . in a way. Blamed. Ridiculed. 'Doesn't do a whole lot for the ego does it? The world I live in is flat. And my people drop off the sides. Carelessly. Without warning. Without seeing what it'll mean to anyone else. To me. For instance.

Jonathan enters.

JONATHAN. I've done the window. Do you want to have a look?

ROANNA. I'm sure it's fine Jonathan.

JONATHAN. I could take it in tomorrow. Shall I?

ROANNA. We'll see.

PAUSE

We could give you a ring: in the morning.

JONATHAN. I'll stay the night.

LAURA. I don't think so. I'd rather be on my own.

ROANNA. You're welcome to stay with us.

LAURA. No. I don't want to.

PAUSE

MICHAEL. Right then. Are we all set?

ROANNA. I want to say something Laura but it's . . . Don't feel . . . I'm sorry we were here. I mean . . . Don't say 'grubby'. Don't put yourself down. Whatever the . . . you know . . . you were trying to help someone . . . as well as . . .

MICHAEL. The shame is you picked someone who wasn't up to it. He didn't deserve it.

LAURA. What?

MICHAEL. Your help.

LAURA. Did I give him any?

MICHAEL. Has anyone else offered him a jolly nice flat to stay in: pretty central. Paid his bills for a while? Looked after him? Tried to get him back on his feet? He's managed to go from having a 'nice place' twice to having nothing now. He's a loser. He's got it written all over him.

LAURA. So he deserves to be shunned?

MICHAEL. He's . . .

LAURA. Not worth it?

PAUSE

I *did* want to help him . . . 'as well as' . . . All this deserving and undeserving stuff is crap. Eddie doesn't deserve to not have as much as he hasn't. Nobody does.

MICHAEL. Why's it up to you to take these . . . unfortunates on board?

LAURA. 'Middle-class guilt.'

MICHAEL. For God's sake!

LAURA. You'll never understand Michael. You never get your hands dirty. You're not involved are you?

MICHAEL. In what?

LAURA. Anything. You're above it all. It's all happening somewhere else. Over there. You pay your taxes and you're exempt. You're a good citizen because you pay your taxes. You *have* to pay your taxes. You pay them. That's you off the hook. If people don't, if they are a mess, in a mess . . . that's their fault. I don't know if it's Eddie's fault. But . . . it's happening everywhere.

MICHAEL. Things have always Never Been Worse.

LAURA. So: don't go too near the fire, you might get burnt.

PAUSE

ROANNA. I'm not like you Laura: I can't take on the world's unfortunates. I imagine I can. I love reading about terribly good people in books or magazines or silly little articles somewhere. I am so relieved there are these saintly people. They are so terribly, terribly good all those people who open their doors and take in

61

people's hell. I dream about being one of them myself. I buy a ticket to somewhere. I get the address. I get a map and I find it and I go and knock on the door and someone opens it and the abused children run into my arms and they come and live with me. And I transform the whole place: jolly, colourful, happy-go-lucky dormitories. And they learn to read. And they eat properly and drink orange juice. And they look forward to the joyful life their very existence entitles them to. And I can think that in a few idle, comfortable moments putting on a wash. I am a unique person exactly as I am. Like this. But saintly. And I'm not. At all. I can get completely beside myself at the thought of Imogen coming in and demanding one and a half minutes of my time. I don't like her being in our street let alone next door. That's how charitable I am. But you try. You do. And I take my hat off to you.

PAUSE

MICHAEL. How much do you think I pay in income tax?

LAURA. I've no idea.

MICHAEL. Guess.

LAURA. Not now Michael. I'm . . .

MICHAEL. It's quite a sum.

LAURA. I'm sure it is.

BLACKOUT

SCENE THIRTEEN

Michael's house. Half an hour or so later.

Michael, Roanna and Jonathan are still in their coats. Imogen is
    distributing her Christmas cards.

IMOGEN. These are in date. For the twelve days. Still valid. Michael.

She hands Michael a card.

Everything will be coming down soon of course. Even the lights in
    Regent Street. Did you see them? I didn't manage to this year. I had
    a quiet Christmas away. Rebecca.

She hands Roanna a card.

Some very nice food. You don't mind being disturbed this early? But
    I do want to get my cards in on time. 'So much better in
    summertime when you no longer have to get up in the dark.'
    Jonathan.

She gives Jonathan a card.

JONATHAN. Thanks.

IMOGEN. Do you like it?

Jonathan opens the card and looks at it.

JONATHAN. Yes. Thankyou.

62

IMOGEN. Read it out.

Jonathan hesitates.

    I chose it specially.

JONATHAN. (reads) 'Peace On Earth. Good Will Toward Men'.

    PAUSE

IMOGEN. And?

    PAUSE

    Don't be shy.

JONATHAN. The message from you?

IMOGEN. Go on. Go on. Go on.

JONATHAN. (reads) 'Get a NICE Girl.'

IMOGEN. And?

JONATHAN. (reads) 'Have some CHEEKY . . . FUN'.

IMOGEN. Yes!

    PAUSE

JONATHAN. Thanks.

IMOGEN. You will!

JONATHAN. Thanks.

IMOGEN. Nice handsome boy. He will. Won't he?

ROANNA. Shall I open my card?

IMOGEN. I'd have him. I'd be his girl.

Roanna opens her card. Glances at it.

ROANNA. Thankyou Imogen. That's very kind of you.

IMOGEN. Has he got one already? Go on. Has he? Have you?

ROANNA. Yes he has.

JONATHAN. No I haven't. (They speak together)

IMOGEN. Big secrets? Little secrets? Big, little secrets. Go on. Did
    you get the sixpence in the pudding?

JONATHAN. Er . . . No, I didn't.

IMOGEN. I'd give you sixpence. If I had sixpence.

    PAUSE

    Why didn't you send me a card? Give me a card. 'To Imogen Jane
    with love and Kissies from Jonnyboy'.

JONATHAN. Um.

ROANNA. You've been away for Christmas.

IMOGEN. Oh yes.

ROANNA. For three days.

IMOGEN. Not too late. Still time. A nice big one with shimmer on it.

'To Imogen Jane with love and kissies from . . . '

PAUSE

Please enclose a signed photograph. With autograph. I could do with some new pictures. I'd *love* a photo of you. Signed across the corner. On the front. Will you?

JONATHAN. Um . . . I don't think I've got one.

IMOGEN. Just a little little one. A little one for my wallet. A passport one.

PAUSE

ROANNA. You'll think about it Jonathan won't you?

PAUSE

But you're not promising.

JONATHAN. No.

IMOGEN. He's my pin-up.

ROANNA. We'll see.

IMOGEN. He sleeps in the dormitory with all the other boys. He should have a girl. Shouldn't he? Some girl to be thinking about him. Quietly. At home. In the dark.

PAUSE

When am I going to come to the school Jonathan and you show me all the rooms properly? The dormitories: with all the boys sleeping together. In their bunk beds. Under the covers. Doing . . . Doing . . . And the rugby lockers. And all the sports. Sweaty sports. Jock straps.

PAUSE

Soon?

MICHAEL. We're all tired at the moment Imogen.

IMOGEN. Tired?

MICHAEL. Maybe we should talk about this in the morning?

ROANNA. I . . .

IMOGEN. It is the morning.

MICHAEL. I mean *later* in the morning.

IMOGEN. You've all got your coats on. Are you going out?

ROANNA. We've just come in.

MICHAEL. And we'd like to go to . . . to turn in now. We're all tired.

IMOGEN. Funny time to be tired.

MICHAEL. Yes. Isn't it?

Michael starts to usher Imogen out.

Thankyou for calling on us and giving us our Christmas cards. We do appreciate it. Whenever they arrive. I'll escort you home.

IMOGEN. Now?

MICHAEL. I'll see you to your door.

IMOGEN. I wouldn't want to put you to any trouble.

MICHAEL. It's no trouble.

IMOGEN. Have a nice day.

Michael and Imogen leave. They continue to talk as they go.

MICHAEL. No trouble at all.

IMOGEN. It's dreadfully kind of you.

MICHAEL. Not at all. This way.

IMOGEN. May I take your hand?

MICHAEL. Of course.

IMOGEN. People rarely are kind.

MICHAEL. Is that so?

IMOGEN. Oh yes!

MICHAEL. I'm sure you're right.

IMOGEN. This is very good of you.

They are out of earshot. Roanna listens. She stops Jonathan from
   speaking.

ROANNA. Sh!

   PAUSE

   Let me see that.

Jonathan gives her his Christmas card. She looks at it.

   I feel quite sick.

   PAUSE

   I *told* you to not get involved. I *told* you you wouldn't know when
   the damned thing was going to end. What on earth are we going to
   do?

Michael enters.

JONATHAN. Sorry.

ROANNA. Are you going to be here when she turns up for elevenses?

   PAUSE

MICHAEL. Yes. I think I'd better be don't you?

JONATHAN. She might not . . .

MICHAEL. If she doesn't, I think you and I are going to have to go
   round to see her. Get this thing straightened out. Right?

JONATHAN. How?

MICHAEL. We tell her you are going to be away for a year . . . You
   are going to be doing your GAP year . . . We tell her you cannot
   have visitors at the school. There isn't any time to have visitors

because you are all working for your exams . . . We tell her you have a girlfriend and her name is . . . what?

JONATHAN. Um . . .

MICHAEL. Anne?

JONATHAN. Yeah.

MICHAEL. Anne! And *she* has your photograph. Okay?

Jonathan nods.

MICHAEL. I'll be spokesman. Okay?

JONATHAN. Thanks.

MICHAEL. If she wants to find out about you she can ask me.

JONATHAN. Thanks Dad. Thanks.

ROANNA. Be careful Michael.

MICHAEL. She's hardly going to get fixated on me Roanna.

ROANNA. She could easily.

MICHAEL. I'm not nearly nice enough. And if she does . . . so be it.

JONATHAN. Thanks Dad.

MICHAEL. Good. So, time to turn in.

JONATHAN. Um . . .

> PAUSE

> Does that mean I can take the GAP year?

MICHAEL. We'd better talk about it hadn't we?

> PAUSE

> Tomorrow?

JONATHAN. Yeah.

MICHAEL. You're going to be here?

JONATHAN. Yeah.

MICHAEL. Good.

BLACKOUT

SCENE FOURTEEN

A park. A few weeks later. Evening.

Laura is waiting. It's cold. She looks at her watch. She looks about her in all directions.

She paces. She looks at her watch again.

Eddie enters.

LAURA. I didn't know if you'd come.

> PAUSE

66

How are you?

EDDIE. I'm here.

LAURA. How's life . . . ?

EDDIE. What do you want?

LAURA. 'Don't mess about do you?'

EDDIE. Come on. It's cold.

PAUSE

Come on! It's cold. The message was you *had* to see me. Here. Now. What do you want?

LAURA. I want to see you. I want to get things right. I want to know how you are.

EDDIE. For fuck's sake!

LAURA. How are you?

EDDIE. How do I look?

LAURA. You look better Eddie. I'm glad.

EDDIE. Good.

LAURA. You're not . . .

EDDIE. Moral lecture now is it?

LAURA. I'm glad you're not mental: we can talk.

EDDIE. What have we got to talk about?

LAURA. Can't you be nice to me? 'How are you Laura?' 'Not bad.' 'That's good'. 'Yeah, not bad.'

EDDIE. Okay. How are you?

LAURA. I'm much better thanks.

PAUSE

I had the worst Christmas of my life. But // I'm getting

EDDIE. (interrupts) So did I.

LAURA. Are you managing to get over it?

EDDIE. No.

LAURA. I'm sorry.

PAUSE

EDDIE. Are you trying to pick me up?

LAURA. Now?

EDDIE. Yeah.

LAURA. No.

PAUSE

But I don't regret for a minute that we . . . I don't. I felt . . . I did buy a dressing gown. It's lovely.

EDDIE. Why were you a cunt when I got back?

LAURA. You were mental.

PAUSE

What did you want from me?

EDDIE. Somewhere to crash.

LAURA. Are you getting yourself sorted out now?

EDDIE. What's it to you?

LAURA. I care Eddie. I do.

EDDIE. She still won't talk to me. I'm taking legal action to get access to my kid. I've got to go back there and get somewhere to live so I can have somewhere for her to come to because the cunt won't let me see her at the flat. Our flat. The flat we got together. The flat that was my home. The flat that she's decided I can't come to any more.

Laura takes an envelope out of her pocket. She hands it to Eddie.

LAURA. I want you to have this.

Eddie looks at it.

EDDIE. What is it?

LAURA. It's the money Michael owes you.

EDDIE. What money?

LAURA. You worked that day for him. I told you I'd get the money for you.

EDDIE. Thanks.

He opens the envelope to have a look, takes a wadge of money out and sees that there is considerably more than the couple of hundred pounds he was expecting.

What is this?

LAURA. I want you to have it.

EDDIE. How much is here?

LAURA. It's about a thousand: a bit over.

EDDIE. I don't want it.

He offers the envelope back to Laura.

LAURA. Please Eddie I want you to have it. If you take it I won't feel, when you turn up again . . .

EDDIE. I'm not going to.

LAURA. If you did.

EDDIE. I won't.

LAURA. I want to part on good terms.

EDDIE. I won't.

LAURA. You might.

EDDIE. I don't want you.

LAURA. I know.

EDDIE. So?

LAURA. I don't actually want you.

EDDIE. So what do you want to give me this for?

LAURA. Look: we're going round and round the houses. You could show up again. You could be in a terrible state. I don't want to feel I should . . . take you in.

EDDIE. I'm not going to give you the pleasure.

LAURA. *If* you 'gave me the pleasure' I'd feel I should . . .

EDDIE. I won't.

LAURA. Will you listen to me Eddie?

EDDIE. You listen to me.

PAUSE

LAURA. I'm listening.

EDDIE. I don't want anything from you. I never . . .

LAURA. You did.

EDDIE. Yeah?

LAURA. Yes you did.

EDDIE. What?

LAURA. You wanted to stay in my flat and you wanted to get into bed.

EDDIE. And you didn't?

LAURA. I did. That's what I am saying. That is what I am admitting. I wanted a little affair. And I wanted to help you out. Yes, I did what I wanted too.

PAUSE

EDDIE. You were ashamed of me.

LAURA. I didn't want to shout it from the rooftops.

EDDIE. Why's that?

LAURA. 'Cos it was a . . . It was never going to be a relationship. It was . . . Men do it to women all the time.

EDDIE. You were using me.

LAURA. And you were using me.

PAUSE

So we were equal.

PAUSE

But you *did* go and publicise it. Even though you'd promised me you wouldn't.

EDDIE. 'Couldn't help it.

PAUSE

LAURA. I wanted you to like me because I was being good to you.

EDDIE. Shit.

LAURA. I know. Total rubbish. I wanted you to stay. You'd like me for that. You'd search for work. I'd support you in that. I'd suggest things. I'd get you bits and pieces to tide you over. We'd get on. We'd have a little affair. Noone would know. I'd feel . . . it was possible for me. We'd like each other. We'd fancy each other. You'd be there at night. Just for a while. Then you'd be gone. That was . . . what I thought would happen.

PAUSE

EDDIE. That is what happened.

LAURA. Yes. But nasty.

EDDIE. 'Cos I showed you up?

LAURA. That didn't help.

EDDIE. I was angry.

PAUSE

LAURA. It turned nasty because it was a silly, naive, half-baked idea.

PAUSE

EDDIE. What do you want? I'm freezing my bollocks off standing here.

LAURA. You say homelessness can happen to anyone?

EDDIE. 'You arguing?

LAURA. No, I'm not.

EDDIE. Good.

LAURA. You don't . . . make it happen to you?

EDDIE. No.

LAURA. You're helpless?

EDDIE. 'You asking me or are you telling me?

LAURA. It's not your fault if you're lonely: it's the same.

EDDIE. Fuck off.

LAURA. It's the same for me. I didn't choose this. Loneliness. It's *my* hole. Did I dig it for myself?

EDDIE. How should I know?

LAURA. I didn't. Loneliness can happen to anyone.

EDDIE. So?

LAURA. I've got sympathy for you. Why can't you find a bit for me?

PAUSE

So we're all cunts?

70

EDDIE. Yeah. And I'm not taking all of this.

He takes the wadge of money out of the envelope.

It was two hundred wasn't it?

He counts that amount out.

LAURA. And about a hundred for your expenses.

EDDIE. I didn't pay that much for the wood: I got a deal.

LAURA. Well Michael's paid that much. So . . .

EDDIE. Right.

He counts out another ninety pounds. He hands the rest back to Laura.

Thanks.

LAURA. Why won't you . . . ?

EDDIE. I'm not a slave.

LAURA. You're not letting me help you.

EDDIE. You can't buy me off.

LAURA. I'm trying to help you. How are you going to get the deposit on a flat if you haven't got any money? I'm offering you the deposit on a flat.

EDDIE. So this is a loan?

LAURA. No. I want you to have it.

EDDIE. What are you trying to do to me? What are you trying to prove? What are you up to?

LAURA. Nothing.

EDDIE. What do you want?

LAURA. Nothing.

EDDIE. What's in it for you?

LAURA. Nothing.

EDDIE. Yeah. And pigs can fly.

LAURA. I don't want anything.

EDDIE. You do want something.

LAURA. Yes I do. I want to like myself when I wake up in the morning. That's what I want. I want to not be lonely. I want to be a good citizen. I want to care. I want to keep my eyes open. I want to put my money where my mouth is. I want to give you this.

PAUSE

Please take it.

She holds the envelope out towards Eddie.

I'm not doing this because I think I should. Okay? I'm doing it because I want to.

PAUSE

EDDIE. Why me?

LAURA. Why not you? You're taking us right back to the beginning. What's the point in that?

PAUSE

EDDIE. It's a lot. For you.

LAURA. It's not a fortune.

PAUSE

Come on: it's getting cold.

PAUSE

Please.

PAUSE

Why not?

EDDIE. So me taking that gets rid of me?

LAURA. If you like.

EDDIE. And makes you feel good?

LAURA. In a way.

EDDIE. Are you mad?

LAURA. Probably.

PAUSE

Eddie takes the money.

BLACKOUT

THE END